A gift for:

_____

From:

_____

★ ★ ★

SEEING GOD IN

★

America

BY LARRY LIBBY

Contents

Introduction

"HOW AWESOME IS THIS PLACE!"

*When Jacob awoke from his sleep, he thought, "Surely the Lord is in this place,
and I was not aware of it." He was afraid and said, "How awesome is this
place! This is none other than the house of God; this is the gate of heaven."*

—GENESIS 28:16-17

When Jacob opened his eyes at sunrise in his sheltered camping spot, the first thing he remembered was the vision that had come to him in the middle of the night. If he lived to be 147 (and he did), he would never forget it. He'd seen a grand stairway resting on the earth near his little camping spot, with the stairs winding up, high through the night sky into the wonder of heaven. God Himself had been standing at the top of the stairway, and countless magnificent angels had been walking up and down the stairs.

Jacob was stunned and shaken by what he had experienced. It was more than a dream; he knew he had seen something real. *God* had been in that place—and he hadn't even realized it.

When he had curled up in his cloak to sleep that night, it had seemed like a perfectly ordinary camping spot. Grass, trees, rocks, crickets, a whisper of wind in the treetops, and a few drowsy night birds. But now . . . after he had seen God in that place, with angels coming and going on the golden stairs, it could never be ordinary again. This wasn't just a random tent site under some trees; it was the very gate of heaven!

What Jacob discovered in the land of Canaan we can discover in America as well. If we catch a glimpse of heaven and experience God's nearness in the places we travel and explore, those places will never again seem ordinary to us.

Instead, they will be threaded through with memories of walking and conversing with Him. We won't be just "seeing America," we will be seeing God in America. And that is a very different proposition.

This little book is like looking through a keyhole at some of the loveliest, most intriguing, awe-inspiring corners of our much-loved nation. You'll see quick glimpses of all fifty states, highlighting some of the most unforgettable cities and towns, panoramic vistas and natural wonders, boundless parks, and scenic highways that seem to ride the top of the world. From the dancing northern lights on a clear arctic night in Anchorage, to the mysterious glowing white sand dunes of southern New Mexico, to the color-splashed autumn hills of the Blue Ridge Parkway in North Carolina . . . No matter which of these places you explore for yourself, God has already traveled ahead of you, scoped out the details, and prepared for your arrival.

Every corner of America and everywhere you go can be a "gate of heaven," if you have eyes to see it. With Jacob, you'll find yourself saying, "How awesome is this place!"

Kansas City, Missouri

CITY OF FOUNTAINS

"For my people have done two evil things:
They have abandoned me—
the fountain of living water.
And they have dug for themselves cracked cisterns
that can hold no water at all!"

—JEREMIAH 2:13 NLT

Back in 1893, the Kansas City Humane Society built the city's first fountain on the corner of Third and Minnesota. It wasn't supposed to be aesthetic. In fact, it was a large square pedestal with four small pools for the benefit of thirsty dogs and horses. People liked it too, however, and somehow the idea of Kansas City fountains caught on and kept growing through the 1890s. The first city-built fountain was dedicated in 1899, at a cost of $42,000. Fountain-building, with its decorative statuary, surged in the 1920s, and building has continued throughout the city's history. Today, fountains form part of Kansas City's identity and honor many of its prominent citizens. While the city itself has two hundred fountains in the Metropolitan area, that number doesn't include hundreds more found on corporate and private property. Only Rome, it is said, has more fountains than Kansas City.

Fountains bring beauty and life to any city. In Scripture, God refers to Himself as "the fountain of living water" (Jer. 2:13 NLT). Jesus said, "Those who drink the water I give will never be thirsty again. It becomes a fresh, bubbling spring within them, giving them eternal life" (John 4:14 NLT). Water, then, is a picture of life—eternal life in heaven and abundant life here on earth. And no matter what our world or culture might tell us, God is the only Source of that life. He is the Fountain, the Headwaters, the Artesian Spring. In Jeremiah's day, people were turning away from God, looking for life in themselves, in their pleasures, in traditions, and in false gods. But all of these attempts were like carrying water in a leaky bucket, and real life just slipped away from them. It's the same with us. We can become preoccupied with many good things—careers, hobbies, politics, recreation, sports, family, and even church responsibilities—but the true source of life never changes. Unless we draw life every day from Jesus, we begin to dry up inside and have little to offer anyone.

Lord, I realize today that I can't refresh anyone else if I don't stay refreshed myself. Please be that clear, beautiful, flowing Fountain in me today.

★ ★ ★

LIVING WATER WILL POUR INTO ME AND OVERFLOW, IF I KEEP THE TAP OPEN.

Bayfield, Wisconsin

GATEWAY TO ADVENTURE

*As he walked along the shore of the Lake of Galilee, he saw two
fishermen, Simon and his brother Andrew, casting their nets into the
water. "Come and follow me, and I will teach you to catch men!"
he cried. At once they dropped their nets, and followed him.*

—MARK 1:16–18 PHILLIPS

Bayfield, Wisconsin, was tailor-made for a travel brochure: a picturesque
small town on a hill (covered with bright foliage in the fall) that slopes
down to a broad beach by a vast blue lake with tall-masted sailing boats in the
marina. What's more, Bayfield's location on the northern tip of the state on
Lake Superior makes it the ideal jumping off place for exploring the nearby
Apostle Islands National Lakeshore with its famous sea-sculpted sandstone
caves. The islands have been called "the jewels of Lake Superior," with lighthouses, hiking trails, bird-watching, and the unique arches, vaulted chambers,
and mysterious passageways offered by the sea caves. Kayakers and boaters
explore the spectacular formations on their own, but daily boat tours are also
available.

The Apostle Islands remind us that the original apostles of Jesus willingly
entered into a life of unprecedented adventure. For two young brothers, Simon
and Andrew, the call of Jesus altered the whole direction of their lives. There
was something about the young rabbi that immediately drew them. His call
so captured them that they dropped their nets, walked away from their business, and gave themselves to a task they had never dreamed they could do. We
too have the opportunity to follow Him today. And it is still an adventure!

Although He may not ask us to walk away from our careers, He has an exciting future itinerary for every one of us, no matter who we are or what has transpired in our lives. Simon and Andrew gave themselves to the great adventure and followed Jesus from that day forward. We too must be willing to surrender our plans and our agendas, in order to embrace opportunities and exploits beyond what we ever imagined for ourselves.

Father, I've been wrapped up in all my own plans and speculations too long. Lift my eyes to see the adventures You have waiting for me as I offer myself each morning to pursue Your will.

★ ★ ★

THE GATEWAY TO ADVENTURE BEGINS WITH ASKING,
"LORD, WHAT DO YOU HAVE IN MIND FOR ME TODAY?"

The Cloisters
New York City, New York

MASTERPIECE IN THE MAKING

*For we are God's masterpiece. He has created us anew in Christ
Jesus, so we can do the good things he planned for us long ago.*

—EPHESIANS 2:10 NLT

The Cloisters museum and gardens is a branch of New York City's Metropolitan Museum of Art and houses a collection of approximately two thousand works of medieval European handiwork. Located in Fort Tyron Park in the Washington Heights area of Upper Manhattan, the Cloisters is situated on a magnificent four-acre viewpoint overlooking the Hudson River. The structure of the museum itself is unique—and a work of art in its own right. Elements from medieval European cloisters were shipped to New York and painstakingly reassembled, stone by stone. The museum's masterworks include illuminated manuscripts, stained glass, metalwork, enamels, ivories, and tapestries. The area adjacent to the building has been landscaped according to medieval patterns, including numerous cloistered herb gardens. From the building to the artifacts, to the setting and the grounds, the Cloisters is a masterpiece among museums.

Today's scripture tells us that we too are masterpieces of God, re-created in Christ to do good works He planned for us long ago. Sometimes in our discouragement, however, we may wonder if God is working in our lives at all. At times it's difficult to imagine ourselves as the handiwork of the living God.

The word in Ephesians 2:10 translated as "masterpiece" is the Greek term *poiema*, from which we get our English word *poem*. We are God's workmanship, His composition, His painting. He truly is at work in our lives, shaping us through circumstances, through difficulties and heartaches, through His Word, and through the counsel of His indwelling Holy Spirit. In Philippians 2:13 (PHILLIPS), Paul reminds us that "it is God who is at work within you, giving you the will and the power to achieve his purpose." As with a partially finished painting, we may not see a pattern or purpose in the seemingly random lines, strokes, and daubs of color. But the Master Artist knows what He is doing. We are His workmanship, His masterpiece, and we are not our own.

Father, by faith I believe that You are working in me right now, creating something and someone You had planned before I was even born.

★ ★ ★

DON'T MAKE TOO MANY CONCLUSIONS ABOUT A HALF-FINISHED PAINTING.

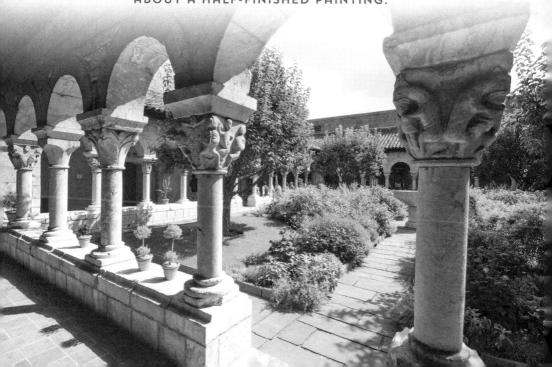

The Liberty Bell Center Philadelphia, Pennsylvania

LIBERTY

*"The Spirit of the LORD is upon Me, because He has anointed Me . . .
to heal the brokenhearted, to proclaim liberty to the captives."*

—LUKE 4:18 NKJV

The Liberty Bell, one of the most familiar and beloved symbols of American independence and freedom, is now housed in the Liberty Bell Center in Philadelphia's Independence National Historic Park. Visitors can view the famous crack running up the face of the bell and perhaps make out the words from Leviticus 25:10 inscribed at its crown: "PROCLAIM LIBERTY THROUGHOUT ALL THE LAND UNTO ALL THE INHABITANTS THEREOF." It is certain that bells rang out joyously at the first reading of the Declaration of Independence on July 8, 1776 (not July 4), and many historians believe that the Liberty Bell was among them. In the years since the Revolution, the bell has been claimed as a symbol by those seeking to end slavery and win the right to vote for women. In the late 1800s, the bell traveled throughout the country and was displayed at fairs and public gatherings in both small towns and great cities. The nation, still healing from the deep wounds of the Civil War, needed a unifying symbol to remind Americans of their common heritage.

The apostle Paul once wrote, "It is for freedom that Christ has set us free. . . . Do not let yourselves be burdened again by a yoke of slavery" (Galatians 5:1). He was specifically writing about those who would impose all sorts of religious rules and human traditions on believers. But these words could also apply to personal habits and attitudes that we allow to enslave us, weigh us down, and steal our joy. If Jesus intended to set us free by His sacrifice for us on Calvary, what are those things that tie us up, that trip our feet and weigh on our hearts? Is it a habit? An addiction? A cynical heart? A hardened attitude? An unwillingness to forgive? An old prejudice? Jesus died for our *freedom*. If we allow anything to restrict us or shackle us to a sad, mediocre life, then we are missing His great gift, paid for at such a high price.

Dear God, show me those areas in my life where I'm still acting like a captive—even though You have set me completely free in Christ.

★ ★ ★

IF I'M A CAPTIVE, IT'S BY MY OWN CHOICE. JESUS HAS SET ME FREE.

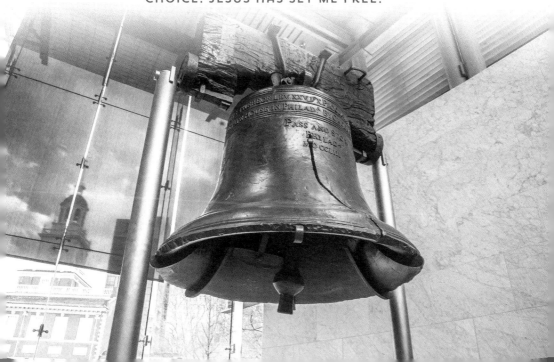

Thorncrown Chapel Arkansas

"REMEMBER ME. . . ."

*"This cup is my blood, my new covenant with you. Each
time you drink this cup, remember me."*

—1 CORINTHIANS 11:25 MSG

Thorncrown Chapel, near Eureka Springs, Arkansas, blends so perfectly with the surrounding Ozark Mountains landscape that it seems to naturally belong there. The chapel's simple lines, soaring beauty, and magnificent setting led the American Institute of Architects to name it fourth on a list of top buildings of the twentieth century. The wood and glass structure with 425 windows, designed by E. Fay Jones, is 48 feet high and constructed with over 100 tons of native stone. It looks like an open-air structure, but is actually enclosed with over six thousand square feet of glass. Thorncrown was the dream of Jim Reed, a retired schoolteacher from Pine Bluff, Arkansas. He commissioned the chapel to give travelers in the Ozarks a place to relax and be inspired. Since it opened in 1980, the chapel has had over six million visitors and won numerous architectural awards. One can assume that by calling the property "Thorncrown," the former schoolteacher's main desire was to honor the One who wore a crown of thorns and gave up His life for our salvation.

Jim Reed gave years of his life and all of his resources to build an unforgettable memorial to Jesus. Only a very few of us, however, will ever have the means or opportunity to create such a monument to honor Christ or to remind us of

His sacrifice. The question remains, however, "What will I do to remember Him?" In John 12:3 we read how Mary of Bethany poured out expensive perfume—possibly her most treasured possession—on the Lord's feet, just before His crucifixion. John tells us that "the house was filled with the fragrance." Jesus said of her, "She did what she could" (Mark 14:8). But what will we do? What will stir our hearts to recall our Savior? We may not be asked to build a chapel or pour out our life savings, but it is good, very good, to remember the cross and what it means to us.

Lord Jesus, the least I can do right now is to think about Your cross, the inexpressible price You paid to save me, and to breathe a word of thanks and praise.

IF MY LIFE IS TOO BUSY TO REMEMBER THE CROSS, IT'S TIME TO RETHINK MY LIFE.

Colonial Williamsburg Virginia

LIVING HISTORY

For whatever was written in former days was written for our instruction, that through endurance and through the encouragement of the Scriptures we might have hope.

—ROMANS 15:4 ESV

You can't really call it a museum. Colonial Williamsburg is more like a living re-creation of one of the most important and dynamic eras of our nation's history. This popular Virginia attraction covers over three hundred acres and includes houses, shops, and public buildings that have been lovingly reconstructed on their original foundations. In addition, the area includes eighty-eight original structures, many open to the public, dating from 1699 to 1780. The idea behind this restoration isn't just to preserve buildings and artifacts; it's an attempt to capture the very atmosphere, flavor, and prominent ideals of this vital era. Visitors may choose either guided or self-guided tours, meeting people in authentic eighteenth-century garb and viewing buildings like the courthouse, gaol (jail), capitol, governor's palace, and individual colonial homes. Along the way, you might encounter famous patriots, listen in on a speech by Patrick Henry, and get caught up in the lives and routines of towns-people, shopkeepers, and political figures.

In the same way, the Bible contains a great deal of history, but is so much more than a history book. In fact, it is alive. The New Testament tells us that "the word of God is alive and active" (Hebrews 4:12). Somehow, though the sixty-six books of the Bible were written through divine inspiration thousands of years ago by different people living in different eras of world history, they all come together in one living, breathing whole. As with Colonial Williamsburg, you can wander the streets, alleys, and pathways of Scripture, pause in open courtyards, peer into windows, walk into different rooms and settings, and find real people interacting with a real God. And everything you see, hear, and touch will have some application for your life now in the twenty-first century. A walk through Williamsburg will interest, teach, and inspire you. A faith-walk through the Word of God may turn your whole life upside down.

Father, thank You for giving me a living Book that speaks to my life today. And thank You for the Holy Spirit, who walks with me as Companion and Guide.

THE BIBLE HAS INSIGHTS THAT REACH INTO ETERNITY—AND THAT ALSO TOUCH THIS VERY MOMENT OF YOUR LIFE.

Skyline Drive Shenandoah National Park, Virginia

THINGS ABOVE

Since, then, you have been raised with Christ, set your hearts on things above, where Christ is, seated at the right hand of God. Set your minds on things above, not on earthly things.

—COLOSSIANS 3:1-2

For a few hours and a little over a hundred miles, you can drive "above it all." America's beloved Skyline Drive runs the entire length of Shenandoah National Park, topping the very spine of the Blue Ridge Mountains of Virginia. Cruising along at the park speed limit of thirty-five miles an hour, the drive could take you three hours—or all day, if you stop at any number of the seventy-five overlooks. Off to the west lies the legendary Shenandoah Valley, and to the east, an undulating landscape known as the Piedmont. In spring and summer, wildflowers spill over the roadsides. In the fall, the roadway soars above a multicolored sea of hardwoods in their glory. At certain times of the year, dense fog settles over the valleys, while the roadway up above winds its way toward bright sunny skies. It may not be a road to heaven, but driving high above the Shenandoah may give you the feeling of leaving anxieties and cares at some turnout in the valleys far below.

At times, the Christian life may remind us of the above/below separation experienced by drivers on Skyline Drive. And here's the paradox: though Christians live out our days on earth, our real and permanent home is in heaven with Christ. Though we claim national citizenship, our true and lasting citizenship is in another place. Though we have to function in a physical world with physical challenges and demands, we're directed to fix our eyes on invisible spiritual realities. In Colossians 3, Paul urges us to set our hearts and fix our minds on a place and time beyond our experience—and literally out of this world. As C. S. Lewis wrote in *Mere Christianity*: "A continual looking forward to the eternal world is not . . . a form of escapism or wishful thinking, but one of the things a Christian is meant to do."

Father, I've given too much attention to the pressures and anxieties of daily life. Lift my thoughts, Lord. Lead me to a vista point where I can catch a glimpse of heaven.

LIFE HERE ON EARTH IS LIKE BACKING OUT OF THE DRIVEWAY. THE REAL JOURNEY IS YET TO COME.

Zion National Park
Utah

BE STILL

"Be still, and know that I am God;
I will be exalted among the nations,
I will be exalted in the earth."

—PSALM 46:10

Up to three million people visit Zion National Park in southwestern Utah each year, filling up guided-tour shuttle buses, hiking along the Virgin River, and snapping pictures at every majestic bend in the road. But in spite of all these visitors and all these sounds, there is a stillness in this place that you can feel.

Rather than looking down from a high rim, as in the Grand Canyon, visitors find themselves looking up at towering sandstone cliffs and mighty monoliths that take on shades of red, pink, and cream in the changing light. The attractions in Zion Canyon have sober, biblical-sounding names: The Narrows, The Grotto, Weeping Rock, Angels Landing, Great White Throne, The Sentinel, and Emerald Pools. At the Court of the Patriarchs, three colossal sandstone peaks named Abraham, Isaac, and Jacob soar into the blue Utah sky, with Abraham the highest at 6,890 feet. Something about the immensity, regal beauty, and grandeur of these formations and natural wonders make you want to stand in stillness, at least for a minute or two, in an attempt to take it all in.

It isn't easy for people of our day to be still. At home we have TV, radios, computers, tablets, and miniature, full-range speakers we can carry anywhere.

Our ever-present smartphones chirp, ding, whistle, and buzz; bring us face-to-face conversations; or endlessly cycle our favorite playlists into earphones. At night cable news drones on and on about a dangerous, mostly unhappy world that unravels more every day. The Lord Himself, however, says, "Be still, and know that I am God." In the original language, the term *be still* could also be translated "cease striving." In other words, set aside all the noise, conflicts, and lesser thoughts that occupy your mind, and remember who He is.

Lord God, You are the sovereign, all-wise, all-powerful Creator and King of the universe. Yet because of Jesus, You allow me to call You Father. For a few brief moments, help me to still my noisy thoughts and consider again who You are and what You have done for me.

★ ★ ★

GOD SPEAKS TO US, BUT CHOOSES NOT TO RAISE
HIS VOICE OVER OUR MANUFACTURED NOISE.

Lilac Festival
Spokane, Washington

THE SCENT OF LILACS

But thanks be to God, who always leads us in triumph in Christ,
and manifests through us the sweet aroma of the knowledge of
Him in every place. For we are a fragrance of Christ.

—2 CORINTHIANS 2:14–15 NASB

Spokane has been known as "The Lilac City" since the 1890s, but the real effort to live up to that title didn't start until the early 1930s. At that time, a group of determined citizens launched a campaign to plant dozens upon dozens of lilac bushes around the city. On May 17, 1938, the Lilac City held its first Lilac Festival and Parade, and the tradition has continued to this day. The first Lilac Queen was nominated and crowned in 1940–another happy custom that has continued for generations of Spokaners. In order to honor the nation's armed forces, the annual lilac parade merged with a military one, becoming the Armed Forces Torchlight Parade, the largest such event in the nation. Lilacs were the perfect choice for this city in eastern Washington state with a hot, arid climate in the summer and a cold winter with rain and snow. Blooming in red, pink, yellow, blue, white, and the traditional purple, lilacs are hardy plants, easy to grow and easy to maintain. Their fragrance, while subtle, is unmistakable and usually reminds people of spring, new life, and love.

The apostle Paul wrote the words about sweet fragrance in today's Scripture verse right after describing a period of restlessness and anxiety in his life

(2 Corinthians 2:12–13). In spite of his uncertainty and inner turmoil, however, he offered praise to God for spreading the "sweet aroma" of Christ in every place he had been. When you are walking with Jesus and filled with God's Spirit, people all around you catch the very fragrance of heaven. As with lilacs, the scent is subtle but unmistakable. You don't have to "have your act together" or be perfectly peaceful and joyful. You might have your share of worries and disappointments. But if you are in fellowship with Jesus, His fragrance will follow you.

Lord Jesus, I know that I can't manufacture Your fragrance in my life. It has to come from relationship with You and time spent with You. And that's my desire today.

THE FRAGRANCE OF JESUS SMELLS LIKE LIFE: SPRING . . .
SUNRISE . . . NEW BEGINNINGS . . . AND HOPE.

Wrigley Field
Chicago, Illinois

ENCOURAGE ONE ANOTHER

*Therefore encourage one another and build each
other up, just as in fact you are doing.*

—1 THESSALONIANS 5:11

Through the long history of the Chicago Cubs in Wrigley Field, there have been some years (well, quite a few, actually) when there wasn't much to cheer about. In fact, in their one hundred-year history at Wrigley, the Cubbies' last World Series was in 1945. They lost. Even so, long-suffering fans keep coming back, year after year. With every new baseball season they say to one another, "Maybe this will be the year."

Wrigley Field is a grandfather among Major League ballparks, second only to Fenway Park in Boston. Wrigley, named for the chewing gum tycoon who purchased the team in 1945, is located in a residential/commercial neighborhood in east Chicago near Lake Michigan. Wrigley Field still makes use of an "old school" hand-turned scoreboard and is the only Major League ballpark to feature fly-ball swallowing ivy-covered walls.

If the Cubs need encouragement, so did first-century followers of Christ. In his letter to a group of beat-up, discouraged believers, the author of Hebrews urged them, "Encourage one another daily, as long as it is called 'Today,' so that none of you may be hardened by sin's deceitfulness" (Hebrews 3:13). You can't miss the emphasis here: encouragement isn't something that happens on occasion, but rather something needed *every day*. If encouragement doesn't happen, the text implies, hearts quickly grow hard and cynical.

How do we exhort and cheer on our brothers and sisters? Anyway we can. With texts, e-mails, notes, phone calls, thoughtful gifts, and one-on-one conversations. It isn't just a "nice thing to do"; it actually breathes life into faltering friends, relatives, and acquaintances. The word *encourage* literally means to breathe courage into another. Through the long years, the Chicago Cubs have valued the cheers and support of their loyal fans. But breathing encouragement into another Christian is more than a game; it's the very essence of our lives.

Lord, You know I get so wrapped up in my own worries and preoccupations that I forget about those around me who could use a good word. Please forgive me for that. I want to be available today for You to encourage others through me.

**WHEN GOD ENABLES US TO LIFT SOMEONE
ELSE, HE LIFTS US AT THE SAME TIME.**

Gettysburg National Military Park
Gettysburg, Pennsylvania

REMEMBER THE BATTLES

"Do not be afraid; do not be discouraged. Be strong and courageous. This is what the LORD will do to all the enemies you are going to fight."

—JOSHUA 10:25–26

In the summer of 1863, the peaceful farming community of Gettysburg in south central Pennsylvania became the scene of the bloodiest battle ever fought on American soil. Over fifty-one thousand Union and Confederate troops died in three days of desperate fighting. Some four months after the fallen soldiers had been buried and the wreckage of war cleared away, President Abraham Lincoln visited the site to dedicate a Soldiers National Cemetery. Lincoln wasn't the main speaker but was asked to give "a few appropriate remarks" at the conclusion. No one remembers the long speech that preceded him, but Lincoln's 266 words have endured through the years as the Gettysburg Address.

Visitors today to the National Military Park can tour the battlefield, view monuments and markers, and walk through the Gettysburg National Cemetery. With so many visitors to the area, developers bought surrounding land and constructed tourist accommodations right up to the edge of the battlefield. The ground made sacred by the sacrifice of so many was in danger of being commercialized. The National Park Service, however, in partnership with many patriotic citizens, pushed back the development, actually reclaiming lands and original features around the area where so many men perished. The fields of Gettysburg have been preserved from the bulldozer because a group of Americans were determined to remember the battle and honor the sacrifice.

In the same way, we must remember the spiritual battlefields of our lives. We need to reflect on those times when we cried out to God to heal a loved one, save a marriage, turn back a wandering son or daughter, or deliver us from some deep trouble of our own making. We need to remember the long nights and the warfare waged on our knees, when we cried out to heaven and God fought the battles we could never have fought on our own.

Father, I do remember times and places when I called out to You with all my heart, and You heard me and helped me. And I know that in my next battle, You will be there again.

MARK THE PLACE WHERE GOD MET YOU IN YOUR NEED. IT IS SACRED GROUND.

West Quoddy Head
Lubec, Maine

ON THE EASTERN EDGE

He has not punished us as we deserve for all our sins. . . . He has removed our sins as far away from us as the east is from the west.

—PSALM 103:10, 12 TLB

You'll never be closer to Europe anywhere within the continental United States than at West Quoddy Head in Maine. Nearby Lubec may claim to be the easternmost town, but the classic, historic lighthouse at West Quoddy is further east still. The original lighthouse was built in 1808, just thirty-two years after America became a nation. In 1820, Congress authorized money to install a five-hundred pound bell at the station that would toll out a warning to nearby ships creeping along the coastline through the fog. The current tower, with its distinctive candy-cane striping, was completed in 1858. Fifteen miles away, across the Lubec Channel, the town of Lubec offers dining and lodging options and all the recreational opportunities you would expect of coastal Maine. These include walking and hiking, bird- (or whale-) watching, fishing, boating, cycling, art galleries, and cross-country skiing and snowshoeing in the winter.

At low tide, you can walk out onto the rocky shelf below the West Quoddy Head lighthouse and stand on the very eastern lip of the United States. If you wanted to see the westernmost point of America on the same vacation, you'd have to drive some 3,700 miles to Cape Prince of Wales, Alaska. It's a long way across a continent, from east to west.

But where, then, is the utter east point of the whole world? You will never find it! The fact is, if you keep going south, you'll end up going north again. But if you travel east, you will never be going west. You'll keep heading east forever. In Psalm 103:12, the Lord tells us that our sins will never catch up with us, nor will we ever meet them again. He has utterly, completely, and eternally removed our sins from us. And that is the unfathomable, immeasurable wonder of the cross.

Father, how good You are to remove all doubt about the return of past sin. Because of Jesus, You have sent my sins away forever. It's almost too wonderful to contemplate. What incredible grace!

★ ★ ★

EAST WILL NEVER MEET WEST. AND WE WILL NEVER IN ALL
ETERNITY BE CONFRONTED WITH OUR FORGIVEN SINS.

The Barrier Islands, Mississippi

SHIFTING SANDS

How do you know what will happen even tomorrow? What, after all, is your life?
It is like a puff of smoke visible for a little while and then dissolving into thin air.

—JAMES 4:14 PHILLIPS

One of the most unique places in the state of Mississippi lies just beyond its beautiful coastline. Stretching nearly eighty miles across the state's Gulf of Mexico shore, a chain of five narrow, elongated islands offer an unusual landscape and a peaceful refuge for those who make the effort to explore them. The islands—Petite Boise, Horn, East and West Ship, and Cat—are part of the Gulf Islands National Seashore Park. Each island has its own unique history, features, and possibilities for relaxation and adventure. All five islands are accessible by private boat and chartered cruises, but only Ship Island offers regular passenger ferry service. Visitors on day trips can choose from a range of activities, including hiking, bird-watching, fishing, kayaking, and snorkeling. Boaters and kayakers, however, are wise to keep an eye on weather conditions, because the islands are always vulnerable to storms blowing in from the gulf. Hurricanes have actually submerged parts of the islands beneath the sea, changing their shapes and shorelines.

Visitors might find these islands to be scenic hidden jewels, but in stormy times no one should place confidence in them as a refuge. Confidence is a positive quality for every Christian—*as long as that confidence rests in God Himself.*

The very best confidence we can have is rooted in the character, wisdom, and power of the Creator. Human abilities falter. Health can change in a heartbeat. Finances can blow away like leaves in the wind. Trusted relationships can fail or be swept away by death. Even loved and respected Christian leaders can stumble. But when we anchor our confidence in the eternal God, we can rest with full assurance. The apostle Paul reminds us that in all the great and unpredictable storms of life, "we are more than conquerors through him who loved us" (Romans 8:37).

> *Father, I need reminding that what seems so solid in my life right now is really only shifting sand. Thank You, God, for a firm place to stand in such an uncertain world.*

SELF-CONFIDENCE WILL NEVER BE ENOUGH WHEN YOUR WORLD TURNS UPSIDE DOWN.

Kennedy Space Center Florida

DOORSTEP OF THE HEAVENS

*When I look up into the night skies and see the work of your fingers—
the moon and the stars you have made—I cannot understand how you
can bother with mere puny man, to pay any attention to him!*

—PSALM 8:3-4 TLB

In 1961, our thirty-fifth president, John F. Kennedy, challenged the nation to put a man on the moon by the end of the decade. That epic feat was accomplished in less than nine years, when Neil Armstrong planted his boot on lunar soil.

When you tour NASA's Kennedy Space Center, an hour's drive from Orlando, Florida, it would be easy to feel very, very small. As you walk through the Rocket Garden you might feel dwarfed by towering launch vehicles from the Mercury, Gemini, and Apollo programs. You can tilt your head back and stare up at the Vehicle Assembly Building, one of the largest buildings in the world by volume and taller than the Statue of Liberty. You can stand under a mighty *Saturn V* rocket, towering 363 feet high—the largest ever made. It would be easy to feel small, insignificant, and over-awed by such colossal structures. Yet even these things are made tiny by the mind-numbing vastness of God's universe.

Even so, the Bible tells us that the Creator Himself, the Son of God, came to our little planet—this "pale blue dot" as Carl Sagan called it—and gave His life for us. The apostle Paul says that "though he was God, he did not think of equality with God as something to cling to. Instead, he gave up his divine privileges; he took the humble position of a slave and was born as a human being. . . . He humbled himself in obedience to God and died a criminal's death on a cross" (Philippians 2:6–8 NLT). He died for us, paying the penalty for our sins, so that we could have a relationship with Him and one day join Him in heaven for eternity. We don't have to feel isolated and lonely in this big universe, when the Creator Himself went to such great lengths to find us, save us, and daily care for us.

Lord Jesus, thank You for caring about me and seeking me out—a microscopic fleck of life on a dust-speck planet.

★ ★ ★

YOU MAY FEEL SMALL AT TIMES, BUT SOMEONE LOVED
SO DEEPLY BY GOD CAN NEVER BE INSIGNIFICANT.

Carlsbad Caverns National Park New Mexico

A CRY FROM A CAVE

Listen to my cry,
for I am in desperate need;
rescue me from those who pursue me,
for they are too strong for me.

—PSALM 142:6

Tucked underneath the scenic Guadalupe Mountains in southeastern New Mexico, the Carlsbad Caverns National Park features one of the largest, most beautiful, and most visited caves in America. The mighty underground complex was discovered in 1898 by a sixteen-year-old cowboy named Jim White. Riding through the brush one day, the teenager found himself at the edge of a huge opening in the ground. He would later write in his book, *Jim White's Own Story*, "Standing at the entrance of the tunnel, I could see ahead of me a darkness so absolutely black it seemed a solid." The caverns, containing 119 known caves, became a national monument in 1923, and were designated a national park in 1930. Some of the underground chambers are up to 250 feet high and contain a vast variety of unusual and colorful formations. Visitors can choose to follow a guide through the lighted caves or take a self-tour.

On the run for his very life, young David sometimes hid from King Saul in various limestone caves in Israel—caves of the same type as Carlsbad Caverns.

The inscription on Psalm 142 reads: *A maskil of David. When he was in the cave. A prayer.* The psalm teaches us that no matter where we are in life, we can call on God and He will hear us. Sometimes when we're depressed, discouraged, or in grief, it can feel like a deep underground cavern. We feel isolated, separated from the world of sunlight, green trees, and fresh breezes. But David felt confident that when he cried aloud, even in those dark depths, the Lord heard him. He went on to pray, "When my spirit grows faint within me, it is you who watch over my way" (v. 3). In other words, even when his life was at its lowest ebb, when life looked its very darkest, he was convinced God had a purpose and a plan for him and would show him which way to go.

Father, sometimes life seems just like a cave—very dark and very deep. But it's so good to know that You are with me, as a Guiding Light, Companion, and Friend.

★ ★ ★

WE MAY FIND OURSELVES IN A CAVE, BUT WE
WILL NEVER FIND OURSELVES ALONE.

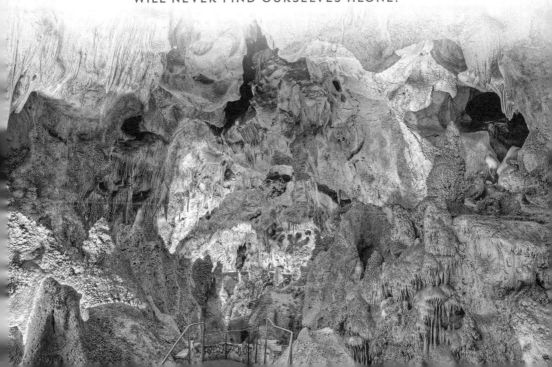

The Three Sisters Mountains Oregon

THREE TOWERING PEAKS

And now these three remain: faith, hope and love. But the greatest of these is love.

—1 CORINTHIANS 13:13

The Three Sisters are a trio of volcanic peaks in the Cascade Mountain Range of Central Oregon, each exceeding ten thousand feet in elevation. Early settlers in the area named the mountains Faith, Hope, and Charity, after the three lofty truths in the final verse of 1 Corinthians 13, the treasured "love chapter." The mountains are one of the most familiar sights on both sides of the Cascade Range and are the third, fourth, and fifth highest peaks in the state. In the winter the three snowcapped peaks catch and reflect the colors of the rising and setting sun, delighting generations of photographers from around the world. The surrounding wilderness and high lakes are immensely popular for hiking, camping, fishing, and climbing. A particular favorite for amateur climbers, the South Sister—Charity—can be ascended in late summer or early fall with no equipment. Sisters, Oregon, the community named for the nearby mountains, is a Western-themed town of over two thousand, and a popular jumping-off point for year-round outdoor recreational opportunities.

When the apostle Paul wrote about faith, hope, and love in 1 Corinthians 13, he probably had no idea he was writing the greatest treatise on love ever penned. At the time, he was bent over a scroll in Ephesus, writing a letter to the very troubled church in Corinth. The fellowship in that wicked city had been torn by immorality, spiritual immaturity, and hurtful divisions. Paul was in the midst of explaining the proper use of spiritual gifts when the Holy Spirit suddenly nudged him down a short side-path. That brief detour became one of the most profound expressions of love in any language. He ended it by speaking of three certainties that will endure when all else fades. He was perhaps saying, "When it's all said and done, dear friends, when life is on the line, there are only three things worth holding onto: your faith in Christ, your hope of heaven, and the love of Jesus as you receive it and live it out in everyday life."

Lord, lift my eyes from so many trivialities to see those enduring mountain-peak truths that make all the difference in life.

★ ★ ★

THREE MOUNTAINTOP TRUTHS—FAITH, HOPE, AND LOVE—
LIFT ABOVE THE FOG AND SHINE WHEN ALL ELSE IS GRAY.

Nome, Alaska

THE FINISH LINE

This is the only race worth running. I've run hard right to the finish,
believed all the way. All that's left now is the shouting—God's applause!

2 TIMOTHY 4:7-8 MSG

It's been called "The Last Great Race on Earth." The annual Iditarod Trail Sled Dog Race begins in Anchorage, Alaska, winds its way northwest through 1,049 miles of some of the most daunting terrain on earth, and ends under a banner on the main street of tiny Nome, Alaska. Along the way, up to sixty sled teams, dogs and drivers, pass through white-out snowstorms, mountains, forests, and tundra—and under the dancing northern lights as darkness falls. The grueling competition launches in early March and runs from nine to fifteen days. The race isn't over until every team has crossed the finish line.

At the race's end, the population of Nome swells by over a thousand people, turning the town into what's been laughingly referred to as the "Mardi Gras of the North." During the two weeks of the race, Nome hosts a basketball tournament, craft fair, art show, dart competitions, and a fierce Nome-to-Golvin snow-machine race.

When the apostle Paul wrote his last letter to Timothy, he described his life as a race just about over. Imprisoned in Rome for preaching about Jesus, Paul knew he would soon be executed for his faith. Life was almost over. "The time for my departure is near," he told his friend. "I have fought the good fight, I have finished the race, I have kept the faith" (2 Timothy 4:6-7).

For Paul, finishing the race meant following his Lord day by day through danger, brutal opposition, hardships, hunger, loss, and loneliness. But with the finish line in view, he must have experienced a great lift in his heart. Jesus was waiting just ahead, friends and saints of old were cheering from heaven's grandstands, and a whole new life was opening up on the other side.

No matter what disappointments, setbacks, and heartbreaks we might experience in our walk with Christ, our greatest priority is to keep our eyes on the goal and to complete the race God has given us to run. What a celebration waits for us just over the finish line!

Lord Jesus, on some days I need strength and stamina beyond my own just to stay in the race. Remind me that the finish line is just ahead, over the river and around a few bends in the trail. Lord, I need a glimpse of You, not only waiting at the end, but also running step-by-step beside me.

IF WE WAKE UP IN THE MORNING AND WE'RE STILL BREATHING, WE HAVE A RACE TO RUN.

Mount Rushmore South Dakota

THE MEASURE OF GREATNESS

"Whoever wants to become great among you must be your servant, and whoever wants to be first must be your slave."

—MATTHEW 20:26–27

Mount Rushmore is a work of art uniquely American in its scope. Where else would you find a vast sculpture with faces over sixty feet high, blasted and carved into sheer granite on the side of a mountain? The massive monument created by Gutzon Borglum and completed after his death by his son, Lincoln, features the likenesses of four American presidents: George Washington, Thomas Jefferson, Theodore Roosevelt, and Abraham Lincoln.

It took fourteen years and four hundred men to carve and shape the mountain—in the midst of a worldwide depression—and was completed in October 1941. Since that time, it has joined the American flag and the Statue of Liberty as the most recognizable symbols of our nation. The sculpture is set in the rugged Black Hills of South Dakota, surrounded by towering rocky crags and dark forests of ponderosa pine and Black Hills spruce. Over three million people each year visit Mount Rushmore National Memorial.

As pleasing as it might be to see your own face chiseled in granite six stories high on a mountainside, there is something infinitely more valuable and enduring than that: it is to become great in the kingdom of God. Those who gain that honor probably won't inspire massive monuments, and you won't find their stories on TV or the Internet. In heaven, however, their fame and renown may be on the lips of angels. In the New Testament, Jesus paid great honor to a nameless woman who broke open an alabaster cask of perfume—perhaps her greatest treasure—and poured it over His head (Matthew 26:6–13). What she did in that moment of selfless sacrifice, Jesus said, would be told in every corner of the world until the end of time. It is the men and women who serve others, quietly, faithfully, with little fanfare, and in the name of Jesus, who attract the attention of heaven.

Father, forgive me for so much concern about being recognized and appreciated for what I do. Help me to give of myself for Your eyes only, out of nothing more than a love for You and a desire to please You.

THE GREATEST PEOPLE WE WILL EVER MEET IN THIS LIFE MAY ALMOST ESCAPE OUR NOTICE.

Amish Country Lancaster County, Pennsylvania

CHOOSING PEACE

Let the peace of heart that comes from Christ be always present in your hearts and lives, for this is your responsibility and privilege as members of his body.

—COLOSSIANS 3:15 TLB

The rich, fertile farmland of Lancaster County, Pennsylvania, is home to America's oldest Amish settlement. Thousands in this community have chosen to live a "plain" lifestyle, much as their ancestors did centuries ago. The *clop-clop* of horses and buggies echo on the roadways, and out in the fields farmers guide horses pulling rakes or plows. Married men are bearded, and both men and women wear nineteenth-century clothing. Visitors to the area might stroll through quaint towns like Bird-in-Hand and Intercourse, take a buggy ride, check out handmade products in multiple cottage industries, or dine on some authentic Pennsylvania Dutch cooking. Devout in their faith, the Amish take seriously the biblical commands to separate themselves from "the world." The most traditional of these groups, the Old Order Amish, don't allow electricity or telephones in their homes—let alone computers, iPhones, or iPads.

The Amish community has chosen to put distance between themselves and our increasingly fast-paced, high-tech, interconnected world. We can learn something from this decision. No, we may not choose to ditch our favorite electronic devices and go back to the 1800s. But we can discipline ourselves to set them aside for a while, to quiet our souls, soak in the music of nature, and converse with the God who loves us. Jesus once told an anxious friend, "Martha, Martha . . . you are worried and upset about many things, but few things are needed—or indeed only one" (Luke 10:41–42). The more we tune in to news, games, gossip, bargains, tweets, posts, stock market totals, and sports scores, the more distracted we become from what truly matters most in life: our relationships with family, friends, and God. We can certainly unplug from technology for an hour or two, or even a full day, to enter into more important communications.

Father, forgive me for putting all my devices ahead of my conversation with You. Strengthen my discipline to walk away from it all for a time, to better hear Your voice and sense Your smile.

★ ★ ★

TOO MUCH INPUT AND TOO MANY VOICES DROWN OUT THE BEST AND WISEST VOICE OF ALL.

Great Smoky Mountains National Park Tennessee and North Carolina

OLD AND NEW

The ancient mountains crumbled
and the age-old hills collapsed—
but he marches on forever.

—HABAKKUK 3:6

Straddling the border between North Carolina and Tennessee, one of America's oldest and most popular national parks offers visitors a wide variety of natural and historical attractions. Up to eleven million tourists travel through the Great Smoky Mountains National Park each year—more than twice the number who visit the Grand Canyon. Visitors appreciate the opportunities for hiking, camping, fishing, bicycling, and simple sightseeing. Cades Cove may be the most popular area of the park. It's a broad valley rich in wildlife, surrounded by mountain peaks, and dotted with faithfully restored buildings and homesteads from the eighteenth and nineteenth centuries, giving visitors glimpses into old-time southern Appalachian life. In 846 square miles of protected parkland spanning two states, there are countless waterfalls, trails, and scenic overlooks for guests who are ready to escape the congested confines of city and suburban life.

Geologists list the Great Smoky Mountains as among the oldest in the world.

Older than America. Older than the Cherokees who once hunted the beautiful hardwood forests. Older than the nameless tribes who roamed the slopes and valleys before them and older than the patriarchs of the Bible. The mountains are ancient, their once-sharp peaks eroded and rounded by the passing years. But every springtime, God clothes the mountains, forests, and valleys with new growth on trees, fresh grass in the meadows, and a glorious profusion of wild-flowers—including delicate trilliums, mountain laurel, wild rhododendrons, and flame azaleas. It's a reminder that though we face old problems, long-term challenges, or ongoing difficult situations, God's strength, help, wisdom, provision, and store of creative ideas and solutions are available with every sunrise. Those who seek Him in the early hours of the day will find that His mercies are "new every morning," and that He brings fresh plans and a fresh provision of strength (Lamentations 3:23; Isaiah 40:31).

Father, thank You that You are the God of the new. In You, Lord, there is new grace, new help, new guidance, new inspiration, and new energy for everything I will encounter today.

★ ★ ★

GOD HAS FRESH ANSWERS TODAY FOR YOUR
OLDEST, MOST DIFFICULT LIFE SITUATIONS.

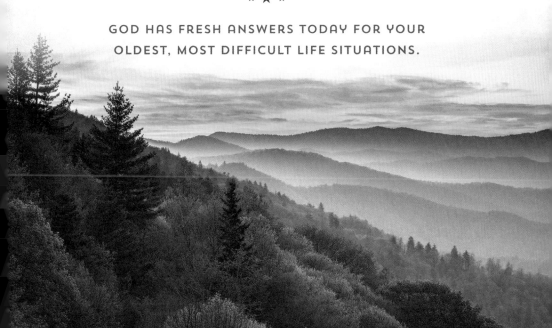

Mount McKinley Alaska

THE GREAT ONE

You faithfully answer our prayers with awesome deeds,
O God our savior.
You are the hope of everyone on earth. . . .
You formed the mountains by your power
and armed yourself with mighty strength.

—PSALM 65:5-6 NLT

They're called "The Thirty Percent Club." These are the 30 percent of visitors to Mount McKinley who actually see the towering mountain peak instead of the clouds that usually shroud it from view. Alaska summers are often drenched with rain, and this mountain is so massive that it creates its own weather patterns. Mount McKinley (also known as Denali, or "The Great One," in one of the native tongues) is the highest mountain in North America. Denali National Park, which includes Mount McKinley, covers six million acres filled with wildlife, boundless unfenced lands, and the unmatched tranquility and solitude of a vast wilderness. The park is located in the Alaskan Range about 170 miles southwest of Fairbanks. In spite of its remoteness, more than 425,000 people make the trip every year, looking for that elusive glimpse of one of the greatest mountain peaks in the world.

Even though odds are against a clear view of the peak, people still come, waiting and hoping for that break in the clouds when they can fill their eyes with the Great One, the High One, the most grand and glorious mountain in the United States. We need glimpses of such greatness because we live so much of our lives consumed by minutiae. We become overwhelmed by a thousand little problems, frustrations, and personal roadblocks that keep us from living on a higher, more satisfying level. A week's vacation and a glimpse of a mighty mountain can certainly bring some temporary relief to our souls. Spending time with the One who formed Mount McKinley with His own hands, and filling up the eyes of our hearts with a fresh gaze at Him can bring relief that will last a lifetime.

Lord, I want to set aside my problems and concerns for a few minutes to fill my thoughts with Your greatness, Your might, and the awesome reality of who You are. Lord, may the clouds in my mind clear away today because I really need to see You.

MOUNT MCKINLEY—AND ALL MY WORRIES AND
FEARS—SHRINK TO INSIGNIFICANCE
BEFORE THE REAL GREAT ONE.

Chesapeake Bay Bridge-Tunnel Virginia

A QUESTION OF TIME

But you should never lose sight of this fact, dear friends, that time is not the same with the Lord as it is with us—to him a day may be a thousand years, and a thousand years only a day.

—2 PETER 3:8 PHILLIPS

For many East Coast residents, the Chesapeake Bay Bridge-Tunnel may seem like such an ordinary part of the daily commute that it no longer strikes them as a wondrous engineering marvel. Every day, thousands of north- and southbound cars, trucks, and motorcycles drive the eighteen-mile combination of soaring bridge and tunnel between Virginia Beach and the Delmarva Peninsula, linking them to Delaware and Eastern Shore counties in Maryland and Virginia. Who remembers that the fifty-year-old transportation link saves them ninety-five miles and ninety minutes of driving time? First opened in 1964, the bridge-tunnel replaced a time-consuming ferry system in operation since the 1930s. Today, the mighty highway structure is a tourist attraction in its own right, offering sweeping views of the Atlantic Ocean and Chesapeake Bay.

Remarkable engineering triumphs like the bridge-tunnel might save many minutes in the car, but in the end everyone has the same amount of time to live through each day. What we may forget, however, is that though we are bound by time, our heavenly Father is not. God lives in timeless eternity, above and outside of time. And when we are walking in His will, He has ways of helping us beyond all our calculations. This is the God who stopped the sun and moon in the sky so that Joshua's army would have time to defeat the Amorites (Joshua 10:12–15). This is the God who plucked Philip the evangelist from a desert road below Jerusalem and instantly deposited him miles away in a city near the coast (Acts 8:38–40). In short, we can trust God with whatever time we have to do whatever we need to do, and let Him work out the details.

Lord, I yield my limited time and small abilities to You. I trust in You to expand my minutes and bless my efforts to accomplish whatever work You've put before me to do.

★ ★ ★

GOD HAS WAYS OF MOVING US AHEAD IN LIFE
BEYOND OUR DREAMS OR IMAGINATION.

Old Faithful Geyser Yellowstone National Park, Wyoming

FAITHFUL

The LORD is trustworthy in all he promises
and faithful in all he does.

—PSALM 145:13

The Old Faithful geyser in Yellowstone National Park was first brought to public attention after an expedition by explorers in the fall of 1870 in what would become the state of Wyoming. Late one afternoon, as the team rode into an unusual basin, they were startled by an eruption, quite near at hand. One of the explorers later wrote: "Judge, then . . . our astonishment . . . to see in the clear sunlight, at no great distance, an immense volume of clear, sparkling water projected into the air to the height of one hundred and twenty-five feet." The famous geyser, one of the top attractions at Yellowstone, can shoot 3,700 to 8,400 gallons of boiling water from 106 feet to 185 feet in the air, for a duration of 1 1/2 to 5 minutes. Intervals between eruptions vary from 45 minutes to as long as 125 minutes.

Designated a national park in 1872, Yellowstone is mostly within the borders of Wyoming but also touches Idaho and Montana. The park covers 2,249,789 acres of magnificent wilderness and has been a favorite American vacation destination for generations. Visitors come to camp and hike and to witness a vast variety of wildlife and natural wonders—including hot springs and geysers.

Although named "Old Faithful," the geyser really isn't faithful. Intervals between eruptions vary, and the iconic geyser seems to be slowing down. In the 1960s the geyser erupted on an average of every 66 minutes. More recently, though, the average has been every 90 minutes.

As Christians, we daily affirm the faithfulness of our God as His followers did thousands of years ago. David wrote, "Your love, LORD, reaches to the heavens, your faithfulness to the skies" (Psalm 36:5). In other words, "There is no way, Lord, that I can measure or calibrate Your faithfulness to me. How could I, when it reaches higher than I can see, beyond the farthest stars?" In the New Testament, God promises, "Never will I leave you; never will I forsake you" (Hebrews 13:5). Jesus Himself told us, "Surely I am with you always, to the very end of the age" (Matthew 28:20).

Father, even if everything familiar in this life falters, changes, or fails, I know You never will. I give You my trust, now and forever.

★ ★ ★

OLD FAITHFUL REALLY ISN'T FAITHFUL. AND EVEN THE STARS IN HEAVEN WILL FAIL. BUT GOD WILL ALWAYS BE FAITHFUL TO HIS OWN.

Pearl Harbor, Hawaii

SURPRISE ATTACK

Dear friends, do not be surprised at the fiery ordeal that has come on you to test you, as though something strange were happening to you.

—1 PETER 4:12–13

A surprise attack has a way of burning itself into memory. In this century, we think of the terrorist attacks on September 11, 2001. In an earlier generation, millions remembered December 7, 1941, as the most savage, unprovoked assault ever launched against our country. On that day, the empire of Japan attacked the United States Naval Base at Pearl Harbor, Hawaii, bringing America into World War II.

Pearl Harbor is a beautiful deep-water lagoon harbor on the island of Oahu, west of Honolulu, and the current headquarters of the US Pacific Fleet. On that terrible day, the base was attacked by 353 Japanese aircraft in two waves. That morning, in addition to the ships and aircraft destroyed, 2,403 Americans were killed and another 1,178 wounded. The battleship *USS Arizona* and crew were among the first casualties. Today, a gleaming white, 184-foot-long memorial structure rests over the mid-portion of the sunken ship—the final resting place for many of the ship's 1,177 crewmen who perished in the surprise attack. While most people come to Hawaii with sunshine, beaches, and palm trees on their minds, many take time to visit the memorial, honoring those who died with so very little opportunity to defend themselves.

The New Testament clearly tells us that life can be a battle, that attacks will certainly come, and that we may not see them coming. Jesus warns that troubles and personal attacks will come because we belong to Him, Paul tells us not to be unsettled by them, and Peter adds that we shouldn't be surprised when it happens. In other words, don't let surprise attacks—no matter where they come from—throw you. Don't let them knock you off your feet, embitter you, or send you into a tailspin of confusion. Instead, pick yourself up, dust yourself off, and get right back to pursuing the will of God to the best of your understanding. In the end, God will see to it that victory is yours!

Lord, please don't let these unexpected troubles push me off course. Help me to stay on the path You've set before me and continue my walk with You.

★ ★ ★

SURPRISE ATTACKS ARE NO SURPRISE TO GOD. HE ALREADY HAS OUR RECOVERY PLAN IN MIND.

Door County, Wisconsin

THE ORCHARDS COME ALIVE

*But the fruit of the Spirit is love, joy, peace, forbearance, kindness,
goodness, faithfulness, gentleness and self-control. . . . Since
we live by the Spirit, let us keep in step with the Spirit.*

—GALATIANS 5:22-23, 25

*That person is like a tree planted by streams of water,
which yields its fruit in season.*

—PSALM 1:3

When asked to picture the state of Wisconsin, many Americans think of harsh, snowy winters—and possibly huge wheels of cheese. But in Door County, a peninsula in the state's northeast almost enveloped by Lake Michigan, there's much more to the story. Being virtually surrounded by water moderates the county's temperatures, creating a surprisingly pleasant environment for afternoon drives, weekend getaways, long vacations, as well as remarkably productive fruit trees. The 482-square-mile county boasts of more than 300 miles of shoreline, five popular state parks, ten lighthouses, and year-round outdoor recreation. The moderate climate also accommodates a booming cherry industry. Each spring, two thousand acres of cherry orchards and another five hundred acres of apple orchards fill the Door Peninsula with delicate, lacy, pink and white blossoms. In summer, thousands of trees bear millions of pounds of fruit. In 2013 alone, growers harvested over eleven million pounds of sweet and tart cherries.

Each year, spring brings a resurgence of life after a winter's rest. With longer days, shorter nights, and the slow change in temperatures, something stirs within the deepest core of the fruit trees. Blossoms bud and open, and even the oldest grandparent trees in the orchard show fresh pink blossoms and the promise of fruit. With the Holy Spirit resident in our lives, we don't have to wait for a particular season to blossom. Our lives can be a perpetual spring and summer as we increasingly yield to God's Spirit and allow Him to begin blossoming and bearing fruit in and through our lives. It doesn't matter if a person is young or old, a new believer, or if they've known Christ for decades. Giving ourselves over to the divine life surging within us *will* bring beauty, fragrance, and attractive, desirable character traits into our daily experience. It's as sure as May cherry blossoms in Door County.

Holy Spirit, I give up trying to produce beauty or fruit or change of character on my own. I rely on You, working in my life from the inside out to produce that desirable fruit in me.

SPRING BEAUTY AND SUMMER FRUIT COME EVERY DAY
OF CAREFUL, PRAYERFUL WALKING IN THE SPIRIT.

Badlands National Park, South Dakota

THE WALL

With your help I can advance against a troop;
with my God I can scale a wall.

—PSALM 18:28-29

The Wall is a monumental natural barrier, 60 miles long and several miles wide, that extends across a portion of the Badlands National Park in South Dakota. The park itself comprises 380 square miles, and the wall is the backbone, dividing the upper northern grasslands from the southern ones. From the earliest days of travel across the continent, it has been both a landmark and a formidable barrier. Those who view the formation describe it as "unworldly," like an alien city skyline or perhaps a massive stage set sprawling across the landscape that doesn't quite belong. In actuality, it is an extensive set of ridges of sedimentary rock carved into fantastic shapes—sharp pinnacles and spires—by long years of erosion. The park itself, with its moon-like landscapes, deep canyons, jagged buttes, abundant wildlife, and miles of protected wilderness, is a unique American treasure.

South Dakota's geologic "wall" is a natural wonder and a national attraction. But many walls in our lives aren't quite so welcome. As the poet Robert Frost once observed, "Something there is that doesn't love a wall." What is your wall today? What is the discouraging obstacle in your path right now? What is it that keeps you from moving forward into the next twenty-four hours with faith and joy? David dealt with bitter enemies for much of his young life—and through no fault of his own. But on the day he wrote Psalm 18, he woke up with a surge of great confidence in his heart. Yes, he had enemies and no, life wasn't perfect. But on this day, faith and gratitude toward God welled up within him, and he felt like nothing could keep him down. If there was a wall in his path, he wouldn't just "scale" it, he would *leap* over it. When David let faith fill his heart, no obstacle looked too intimidating and no wall too high.

Lord, sometimes I get up in the morning and focus my eyes on walls that hold me back, instead of filling my heart with You, the One who can help me run through barriers and leap over obstacles.

★ ★ ★

**FAITH CHASES AWAY SHADOWS AND
GIVES A SPRING TO YOUR STEP.**

Essex Steam Train & Riverboat
Essex, Connecticut

RECOVERING A SENSE OF WONDER

Satisfy us in our earliest youth with your loving–kindness,
giving us constant joy to the end of our lives.

—PSALM 90:14 TLB

It may be a ride into history, but families who climb on board the Essex Steam Train & Riverboat excursion will be thinking more about present-day fun. The two-and-a-half hour journey begins at the 1892 Essex Station and chugs along at twenty miles per hour through the serene Connecticut River Valley, designated by the Nature Conservatory as "one of the last great places on earth." The beautifully restored steam locomotive and railroad cars pass by meadows, millponds, and farms, as well as the picturesque towns of Deep River and Chester.

On phase two of the adventure, passengers take their leave of the train and board the Becky Thatcher Riverboat for a cruise on the Connecticut River. In the fall, the whole experience turns into an autumn foliage extravaganza, with bright oranges, reds, and golds cloaking the hillsides along the tracks and reflecting off the river. It's an opportunity to set aside grown-up reserve, disinterest, and indifference and be enveloped in a sense of childlike joy and wonder.

In the book of Psalms, David was swept up in wonder when he looked into the night sky. He once wrote: "When I look up into the night skies and see the work of your fingers—the moon and the stars you have made—I cannot understand how you can bother with mere puny man" (Psalm 8:3–4 TLB). Paul bent over backward to help the Philippians embrace joy. He wrote: "Always be full of joy in the Lord; I say it again—rejoice! . . . Don't worry about anything; instead, pray about everything" (Philippians 4:4, 6). It's easy to let endless responsibilities and constant difficulties overtake one's sense of joy, but, with God's help, we can be full of gladness and delight no matter our surroundings or circumstances.

Father, sometimes I take my life—and myself—way too seriously. Help me to remember that I can trust You with the all the details of my world and that You have a great plan for my life. In the meantime, help me to smile more, worry less, and get excited over adventures with my family and Your family.

DON'T LOSE YOUR CHILDLIKE SENSE OF WONDER.
KEEP THE "WOW" GOING IN YOUR LIFE.

Kentucky Horse Park
Lexington, Kentucky

COMPETE WITH HORSES

"If you have raced with men on foot
and they have worn you out,
how can you compete with horses?
If you stumble in safe country,
how will you manage in the thickets by the Jordan?"

—JEREMIAH 12:5

Frankfort, Kentucky, may be the state capital, but Lexington has proclaimed itself "The Horse Capital of the World." The Kentucky Horse Park near Lexington is the pride of a proud commonwealth that revels in its history of producing magnificent thoroughbred horses. The park itself, however, celebrates all breeds of horses–whether elite racehorses worth millions or the hardworking farm animals that meant so much to endless generations all over the world. Open to the public from March 15 through October 31, the park is a 1,224-acre equestrian center and educational theme park dedicated to "man's relationship with the horse." Twice daily, visitors can take in the "Horses of the World Show," which highlights unique characteristics of selected breeds and riders dressed in authentic costumes. The grounds also include the International Museum of the Horse, the largest such museum in the world.

In Bible times, before the advent of missiles, fighter jets, and sports cars, there was no greater symbol of strength, speed, and fighting spirit than the horse. When the prophet Jeremiah complained to the Lord about people and situations in his life, the Lord replied, "If you have raced with men on foot and they have worn you out, how can you compete with horses?" (Jeremiah 12:5). In other words, "If you can't handle the little things, if you can't trust Me for these everyday problems, what will you do when a major crisis crashes into your life?" It's a good reminder for all of us. If our nerves, patience, and faith max out over problems and challenges common to everyone, how will we manage in a major trial or tragedy? The solution, of course, is to bring everything—great or small—to the Lord every day of our lives. As Peter reminds us, "Cast all your anxiety on him because he cares for you" (1 Peter 5:7).

Forgive me, Lord Jesus, for letting worries and fears pile up in my mind and weigh down my shoulders. Help me to trust You—minute by minute—with every situation in life.

**I MAY NOT BE ABLE TO RUN WITH HORSES,
BUT I CAN WALK WITH GOD.**

International Peace Garden
North Dakota & Manitoba, Canada

A PEACEFUL CORNER OF THE WORLD

If it is possible, as far as it depends on you, live at peace with everyone.
—ROMANS 12:18

It may not mean much in the grand scope of international tensions, but the International Peace Garden on the borders of North Dakota and Manitoba, Canada, is a fragrant, beautiful symbol of the peaceful relationship between two great nations that happen to be close neighbors. Established in 1932, the garden exhibits over 150,000 flowers every year. Visitors will see an 18-foot floral clock display, fountains, and twin 120-foot concrete towers straddling the border with a peace chapel at their base. The garden covers 2,300 acres and features two freshwater lakes, hiking trails, wildflowers, waterfalls, and an abundance of North American birds and animals. The sounds of flowing waters can be heard throughout the garden, and every fifteen minutes and on the hour chimes ring out from the Carillon Tower. When the garden first opened, only a pile of stones marked the border, with these words inscribed on a plaque: "To God in His Glory, we two nations dedicate this garden and pledge ourselves that as long as men shall live, we will not take up arms against one another."

It might be easy to discount the relevance of a 2,300-acre botanical garden linking the border of two nations that have been at peace for many years. But in a world with so much violence, threat, mistrust, and cynicism, a peace garden seems like a valid expression—and one that should be heeded by others. The New Testament calls us to live peaceful lives whenever possible with those around us. This won't guarantee tranquility, because we live in an imperfect world with many unhappy people who are determined to make trouble—and particularly for followers of Jesus Christ. But Paul tells us to live in peace the best we can, making sure we don't initiate trouble with others. The apostle Peter adds these words: "Snub evil and cultivate good; run after peace for all you're worth. God looks on all this with approval" (1 Peter 3:11–12 MSG).

Holy Spirit, please stop me from starting arguments, sparking disputes, making negative comments, or taking actions that I know will upset the peace.

★ ★ ★

**WITH GOD'S HELP, MY HOME AND MY WORKSPACE
CAN BE PEACEFUL ISLANDS IN A TENSE WORLD.**

Outer Banks North Carolina

AVOIDING SHIPWRECK

Cling to your faith in Christ, and keep your conscience clear. For some people have deliberately violated their consciences; as a result, their faith has been shipwrecked.

—1 TIMOTHY 1:19-20 NLT

The Outer Banks off the coast of North Carolina are prized as a vacation paradise, with interesting histories, stunning beaches, plentiful sunshine, and welcome quiet and solitude. Visitors to this far eastern fringe of the nation like to wade in the surf, search for seashells, ride a surfboard (or a horse), or just park a comfortable beach chair in the sand and read a book.

But the area has also been known from earliest days for something that may not show up in the tourist brochures: *Shipwrecks.* This chain of barrier islands jutting off the coast and linked by a series of bridges has been a disaster zone for thousands of unwary ships sailing along the Atlantic Coast. Off Cape Hatteras alone, more than one thousand ships have been lost. The first recorded vessel to crash into the Outer Banks was an English ship in 1535, but countless unfortunate ships have followed—victimized by strong currents, hidden sandbars, and stormy seas.

The apostle Paul knew a few things about shipwrecks. When he wrote to the Corinthians, he reminded them that he had been shipwrecked three times in his ministry travels—and once spent a long night and the next day in the open sea (2 Corinthians 11:25). Paul used that term *shipwrecked* to describe the faith of those who had become sloppy and careless with their lives. He was speaking of people who had relaxed their grip on the truth and ended up smashing their faith on unseen hazards. Paul reminded Timothy not to take his faith in Christ casually and not to become careless. The truth is, any one of us could let down our guard and end up on the rocks or stuck in the sand. Paul's counsel? Take a fresh grip on your faith in Jesus Christ, keep a clear conscience, and don't let yourself slip back into old and destructive patterns of life.

Lord Jesus, please give me the strength, discipline, and desire to stay alert and hold on to my faith in You, knowing that You also hold on to me.

THOSE WHO CLING TO JESUS IN CALM WEATHER WON'T LOSE THEIR GRIP IN A SUDDEN STORM.

River Walk
San Antonio, Texas

WALK IN LOVE

Follow God's example, therefore, as dearly loved children and walk in the way of love, just as Christ loved us and gave himself up for us as a fragrant offering and sacrifice to God.

—EPHESIANS 5:1–2

America has all manner of paths, boardwalks, walkways, lanes, and wilderness trails for walking, hiking, jogging, or strolling. The paths may be dirt, cement, asphalt, grass, gravel, sand, or sheer rock. But surely one of the most engaging of those classic American walks must be one that follows the San Antonio River for a thirteen-mile stretch through the heart of sunny San Antonio, Texas. It's called the River Walk, or *El Paseo del Rio*. Along this unique river pathway, visitors and locals alike explore shops, dine in favorite restaurants, stay in nearby hotels, tour museums, and even take short side trips to the famous Alamo or other downtown attractions in America's seventh largest city. If you prefer, you can take to the river itself for a thirty-five-minute boat tour in which guides describe the attractions and the history of *El Paseo del Rio*.

Your walk with God began the day you received Christ as Savior and Lord. But the only part that really matters right now is your walk with God *today*. The Bible calls us to "walk in the way of love," remembering how Jesus loved each one of us, giving up His very life for us. The way of love is the way of sacrifice—of putting others before yourself. Imagine you come to a fork in the road.

One way pleases you and meets your own wants and needs, and the other way lets go of these to help, encourage, serve, or provide for another. On the walk of love, you make the second choice, time after time, remembering what was surrendered for you. Self-sacrifice may sound like a bleak, narrow, joyless kind of walk, but it isn't. Over time, it's a walk filled with light, joy, laughter, productivity, and deep satisfaction. And best of all, it pleases God.

Lord Jesus, I want a walk of love, but I get distracted and pulled away by my own pursuits. Please help me to follow You a little bit longer and a little bit closer on this way of love.

★ ★ ★

EVERY NEW DAY IS THE FIRST DAY OF A WALK WITH JESUS.

Haystack Rock
Cannon Beach, Oregon

A MIGHTY ROCK

The LORD is my rock, my fortress and my deliverer;
my God is my rock, in whom I take refuge, . . .
my stronghold.

—PSALM 18:2

In 1805, after traveling over 3,700 overland miles across the largely unexplored American continent, Captain William Clark, one of the leaders of the Lewis and Clark expedition, saw a great monolith rising up out of the blue Pacific surf and called it "the grandest and most pleasing prospects which my eyes ever surveyed, in front of a boundless Ocean."* Many others have said something similar. Haystack Rock, on the north Oregon coast, is a basalt sea stack towering 235 feet over the beach. It has been called the third largest "intertidal" (meaning that it can be reached by land) freestanding rock in the world. Most photos of nearby Cannon Beach, a picturesque village and year-round vacation destination, include the silhouette of the mighty Haystack. As many as two hundred thousand people visit this million-pound rock every year, taking countless photos, peering into the many tide pools at its base, or watching the thousands of nesting seabirds nearby.

In the Psalms, David frequently refers to the Lord as "my Rock." Why

---

* http://en.wikipedia.org/wiki/Cannon_Beach,_Oregon

was that picture so compelling to him? What was it about a great rock that prompted David to think about God? It may have been several things. First, a rock is *solid*. It will hold you up and won't give way beneath your feet. Second, a great rock is *enduring*. Many other things may change around you, but the rock will remain the same. Third, a huge rock is *a reliable landmark* that will stand for thousands of years. It will remain an anchor point in your world, giving direction and perspective. With all the uncertainty and betrayals in David's life, he longed for the strength and stability of a close relationship with the God of Israel. In the same way, Paul identifies Christ as Israel's spiritual rock in 1 Corinthians 10:4. And He is ours as well. We may not feel steady or stable in ourselves, but with feet planted on the mighty Rock, we will find the strength and staying power we need in every life situation.

Lord, You truly have been the great Rock in my life. Seeing You on the horizon of my life is a comfort beyond words.

★ ★ ★

CHRIST THE ROCK TOWERS HIGH OVER MY GREATEST UNCERTAINTIES.

The White House Washington, DC

THE LEADER WHO STAYS

But about the Son he says,
"Your throne, O God, will last for ever and ever."

—HEBREWS 1:8

The House at 1600 Pennsylvania Avenue is the most famous and recognizable residence in America. For two hundred years, the White House has not only represented the presidency and the executive branch of the United States government but has also served as a personal residence for the current president and his family. Enclosed by a security fence, the White House and grounds cover eighteen acres of land. The residence itself has 132 rooms, 32 bathrooms, and six levels. Some residents of the mansion have found living there an overwhelming experience. Grover Cleveland, the twenty-fourth president, is said to have commented, "Sometimes I wake at night in the White House and rub my eyes and wonder if it is not all a dream." Harry Truman, however, called it "the finest prison in the world."

At this writing, there have been forty-four men who have served as president. While presidents, kings, dictators, and prime ministers serve limited terms of time in office, there is one King whose seat of power has no termination date. The angel Gabriel told Mary of Nazareth that she would bear a son who would become king and whose reign would last *forever*. His kingdom would *never end* (Luke 1:30–33). There is only one King who lives and reigns forever, and that is Jesus, Son of the living God. Israel and Judah had been ruled by forty-two kings and one queen. The evil Manasseh reigned the longest, for fifty-five years. Zimri lasted seven days. The longest-serving U.S, president was Franklin Roosevelt, who served three terms in office before the limit of two four-year terms was instituted. Jesus, however, will reign over Israel—and all creation—for eternity. He will never step down, never be assassinated, never resign, never be overthrown, and never be voted out of office. Eternity will be ever sweeter knowing that the leadership question has been settled *forever*.

King Jesus, someday everyone will bow down before You. But it's such an incredible privilege and honor to love You and serve You now, even when so many people reject You and hate Your name.

★ ★ ★

EVERY LEADER IN ALL THE WORLD IS ON BORROWED TIME. KING JESUS TRANSCENDS TIME.

Mall of America Bloomington, Minnesota

THE MARKETPLACE

While Paul was waiting for them in Athens . . . he reasoned in the synagogue with both Jews and God-fearing Greeks, as well as in the marketplace day by day with those who happened to be there.

—ACTS 17:16–17

The Mall of America in Bloomington, Minnesota, is the ultimate shopping experience. It has also developed into one of the country's top tourist destinations, attracting forty-two million visitors every year. It's been called "a city within a city," and as you attempt to take it all in on a given day, it's easy to see why. Within its expansive walls are over 520 stores, 50 restaurants, and dozens of other attractions, including a theme park with 24 rides, miniature golf, zip lines, movie theaters, flight simulators, and a comedy theater. The multilevel mall covers over ninety-six acres and includes two seven-story, free-parking garages. During Minnesota's icy winters, the mall remains a light, bright, secure place for people to meet, shop, dine, play, and spend time together. In many ways, the Mall of America is like a national marketplace.

The apostle Paul frequented marketplaces in his travels as well. In Acts 17:18, we read that he reasoned with people he met in the Athens marketplace, declaring "the good news about Jesus and the resurrection." "The marketplace" of our lives is where we live, work, shop, run errands, eat dinners out, and attend classes. It's where the people are. It's where men and women interact, complete transactions, and sometimes voice opinions. Paul made sure to include his faith in Jesus in such places, and although some people sneered at him (v. 32), others wanted to know more. Wherever we go as believers in Christ, we need to bring our message of positive life transformation. It doesn't necessarily mean preaching in the streets, but rather giving a simple account of all that God has done for us. The apostle Peter put it like this: "Always be prepared to give an answer to everyone who asks you to give the reason for the hope that you have. But do this with gentleness and respect" (1 Peter 3:15).

Lord Jesus, help me to be ready to speak at the right moments about what You have done to bring such peace and purpose into my life.

ASK THE LORD FOR OPEN DOORS AND YOU'LL
BEGIN TO SEE THEM EVERYWHERE.

Arlington National Cemetery
Arlington, Virginia

REMEMBER THE SACRIFICE

"Greater love has no one than this: to lay down one's life for one's friends."

—JOHN 15:13-14

Looking out across the rolling wooded acres of Arlington National Cemetery, with its hundreds of thousands of white stones in perfectly ordered rows, brings an assortment of emotions that are impossible to escape. Sadness. Desolation. Pride of country. Anger over so many lost young lives. The stones represent tremendous loss as well as the gift of freedom we are able to enjoy.

Arlington National Cemetery is a United States military cemetery located across the Potomac River from Washington, DC, in Arlington County, Virginia. Within its 624 acres, over four hundred thousand active-duty service members, veterans, and their families have been buried. In addition to the military heroes, Arlington is also the final resting place for a select number of presidents, astronauts, senators, and Supreme Court justices. Founded during the dark days of the Civil War, the cemetery now contains the remains of military personnel from every American war—from the Revolution to Iraq and Afghanistan.

But what about those of us who have never been called upon to lay down our lives in battle? Is the whole concept of "sacrifice" something for others and not for us? No! The Lord Jesus Christ calls each of His followers to a *life* of sacrifice, for His sake. The apostle Paul wrote, "Follow God's example, therefore, as dearly loved children and walk in the way of love, just as Christ loved us and gave himself up for us as a fragrant offering and sacrifice to God" (Ephesians 5:1–2). Sacrifice isn't just some dramatic final act of heroism. Sacrifice is also laying down our privileges, benefits, and pleasures for the good of someone else. The book of Hebrews says, "Do not forget to do good and to share with others, for with such sacrifices God is pleased" (Hebrews 13:16). We may yet be called on to give up our lives on earth for the sake of another. But in the meantime, Jesus calls us to daily follow Him by giving more attention, care, love, time, and help to others than we give to ourselves.

Lord Jesus, sometimes my sacrifices seem so small, so insignificant, compared with those who have given so very much. But my goal today is to follow You with all my heart, being ready to set aside my own plans and pleasures whenever You call me to.

SACRIFICE IS A DAILY DETERMINATION TO PUT THE NEEDS OF OTHERS BEFORE OUR OWN.

Crater of Diamonds State Park
Murfreesboro, Arkansas

DIAMONDS IN THE DIRT

If you call out for insight
and cry aloud for understanding . . .
and search for it as for hidden treasure,
then you will understand the fear of the LORD
and find the knowledge of God.
For the LORD gives wisdom.

—PROVERBS 2:3–6

Crater of Diamonds State Park, near Murfreesboro, Arkansas, is the only diamond-producing site in the world open to the public. For a few dollars, you can search over a 37 1/2-acre plowed field for real diamonds and other semiprecious stones. From then on, it's "finders keepers." Whole families come to the park with shovels and buckets, screens and sifters, spending a few hours or all day digging in the dirt—and sometimes going home with real white, brown, and yellow diamonds to show for it.

Most of the diamonds are very tiny with no commercial value. But not all of them! Individuals have found some famous stones, including the 3.03-carat Strawn-Wagner Diamond, picked up in the park in 1990. After it was cut, it was graded D Flawless, the highest grade a diamond can achieve. Diamonds are there to be found, but it takes a little time and effort.

The Bible says that God's wisdom is far more valuable than silver or gold or precious stones. In fact, "Nothing you desire can compare" (Proverbs 8:11). What's more, if you want that wisdom, you *will* find it. The Bible makes it clear that the priceless, private, personal counsel of your Creator, the One who knows you better than you know yourself, is available, free of charge. But you have to want it. The apostle James wrote: "If you need wisdom, ask our generous God, and he will give it to you. He will not rebuke you for asking" (James 4:5 NLT). He will share His thoughts with you in ten thousand different ways. You may not receive the answers you anticipated, and it may take you in a direction you never dreamed, but if you want the wisdom of God and nothing else will do—He'll give it to you.

Father, I know that many times I have walked right by beautiful diamonds of Your wisdom. Open my eyes, Father, and awaken my heart to hear and respond to Your counsel today.

GOD'S WORDS OF COUNSEL ARE BRIGHT,
MULTIFACETED DIAMONDS—AND THEY ARE
AVAILABLE TO THE ONE WHO SEEKS THEM.

The Flume
New Hampshire

UNCERTAIN FOOTING

But as for me, I almost lost my footing.
My feet were slipping, and I was almost gone.

—PSALM 73:2 NLT

Many of America's most sweeping and dramatic natural attractions were discovered by rugged, wide-ranging explorers accompanied by Native American guides. But it wasn't that way for the magnificent Flume Gorge in central New Hampshire. In fact, ninety-three-year old Aunt Jess Guernsey came upon the gorge accidentally in 1808 while she was fishing. Aunt Jess could hardly believe her eyes, but when she related her discovery to her family, they didn't believe her. Finally, she convinced them to come see for themselves. The Flume is a natural gorge extending eight hundred feet at the base of Mount Liberty in the 6,700-acre Franconia Notch State Park. Racing and crashing through the gorge, the Flume Brook is surrounded by sheer granite walls towering seventy to ninety feet high. Guests can choose from a hike through the gorge alone or a longer, two-mile scenic loop. Walking trails follow the stream, but the way can be slippery. Officials at the park recommend proper footwear in order to keep secure footing on the path and the stairs.

The Bible uses the metaphor of walking in slippery, hazardous places to warn us about perils in the spiritual life. The apostle Peter was stern, telling believers that keeping the wrong company could cause them to slip away

(2 Peter 3:17). The psalmist said that his bitterness over God's dealings almost sent him over the edge (Psalm 73:2). Solomon told us to "Give careful thought to the paths for your feet" and by all means to stay on the path! (Proverbs 4:26–27). The point is, the pathway through this life to heaven is not only narrow; it can also be slippery, uneven, or choked with roots and stones. We can't simply stroll along looking at the clouds, trees, and flowers; we have to watch where we place our feet. How do we do that? By saturating our minds with the light and wisdom of God's Word, by praying often, and by staying daily attuned to the voice of the Holy Spirit and His leading.

> *Father, I know that life is short and that stepping off Your path can be dangerous and deeply hurtful. Help me to be vigilant and wise while following Your lead. Remind me to watch where I place my feet.*

★ ★ ★

THE CHRISTIAN LIFE IS BEST LIVED ONE
CAREFUL STEP AT A TIME.

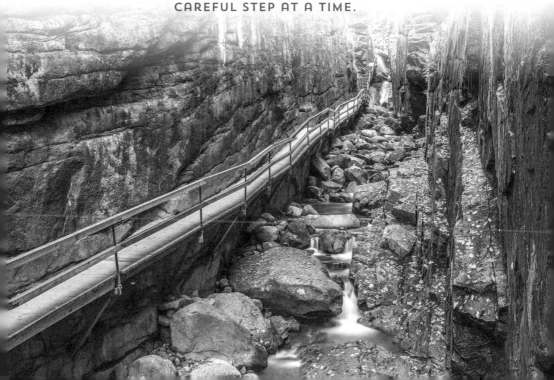

Siesta Key Beach, Florida

PURE REST

Yes, my soul, find rest in God;
my hope comes from him.

—PSALM 62:5

*M*ost everyone has a favorite beach somewhere—a spot they can picture in their mind's eye when the pressures of life mount up and seem overwhelming. It might be in California, Hawaii, South Carolina, or Texas, but it is the place where weary people go in their imagination when they long for a little rest. In the continental United States, one eight-mile stretch of sugary white sand on Florida's Gulf Coast has several strong factors to recommend it. Siesta Key Beach near Sarasota was rated as the number-one beach in the United States by "Dr. Beach," director of Florida International University's Laboratory for Coastal Research. A number of years ago, the Travel Channel proclaimed Siesta "the best sand beach in America"—and for good reason. The white sand is 99 percent quartz, making it cool to the skin even when the temperature soars. Shallow water depth near the shoreline and year-round lifeguard protection make it a safer beach for whole families, giving parents one less worry and one more reason to relax.

God never intended us to work and worry ourselves into a constant state of frenzy. In the Psalms we read: "It is useless for you to work so hard from early morning until late at night . . . for God gives rest to his loved ones" (Psalm 127:2 NLT). After hours of exhausting ministry, Jesus said to His followers, "Come with me by yourselves to a quiet place and get some rest." (Mark 6:34).

This speaks to us of some downtime, some quiet time, some days when we break away from the normal demands of our workday life. On another occasion, Jesus said, "Come to me, all you who are weary and burdened, and I will give you rest . . . you will find rest for your souls" (Matthew 11:28–29). This is the deep relief and overflowing peace we experience when we fully trust Jesus Christ for the forgiveness of our sins, for our standing before a holy God, and for our hope of heaven to come. It's a rest that is with us always and doesn't depend on white beaches and sunshine.

Lord, help me to rest today in Your love, in Your provision for my life, and in Your promise to be with me always.

★ ★ ★

ULTIMATELY, REST ISN'T ABOUT A PLACE, IT'S ABOUT A PERSON.

The Four Corners Monument Arizona, New Mexico, Utah, Colorado

WHEN LIFE LINES UP

He is before all things, and in him all things hold together.

—COLOSSIANS 1:17

There is only one location in America where you can place yourself in four states at the same moment. At the Four Corners Monument, a Navajo Nation park, you can place one hand in Utah, one hand in Colorado, one foot in Arizona, and the other foot in New Mexico. The monument is located in a remote area off of US Highway 160, within Native American land. Navajo (or Dine) and Ute people live in the Four Corners area and display their handmade jewelry, crafts, and food at the monument. Nearby scenic attractions include Monument Valley, the Canyon de Chelly National Monument, and the Trail of the Ancients, a National Scenic Byway passing through territory where Puebloans lived for many generations before European settlement.

At the Four Corners, four important borders converge. Likewise, sometimes life can do the same—several separate streams come together, and you find yourself at the right time, in the right place, meeting the right person or encountering the right opportunity. Those who don't know or believe in God attribute such moments to chance, coincidence, karma, or a lucky break. Those who have a personal relationship with the God of time and eternity, however, know better. It is God Himself who weaves threads of circumstances together into a perfect tapestry. No detail escapes Him. No threads are left hanging. We are told, "A man's heart plans his way, but the LORD determines his steps" (Proverbs 16:9 HCSB). Paul declares, "We know that all things work together for the good of those who love God: those who are called according to His purpose (Romans 8:28 HCSB). No matter how feverishly we might try, we could never cause favorable events and outcomes to converge in our lives. But as we live day by day in Him and for Him, trusting His Holy Spirit to guide our steps, God will bring the strings together at the right time, to help and bless us, and ultimately to advance His kingdom.

Lord Jesus, I look to and depend on You, knowing that You hold my life together and work out everything for my ultimate good.

"I'M SO GLAD I DON'T HAVE TO BE MY OWN TOUR GUIDE THROUGH LIFE."—PASTOR RON MEHL

Virginia City, Nevada

SILVER AND GOLD

Your instructions are more valuable to me
than millions in gold and silver.

—PSALM 119:72 NLT

*V*irginia City seemed to spring up overnight in southwest Nevada with the 1859 discovery of the Comstock Lode. This was one of the most important mining discoveries in American history and the nation's first significant silver deposit. By the mid-1860s, while the Civil War raged in the East and South, the population of Virginia City had soared to twenty-five thousand residents. Proceeds from the mines amounted to millions of dollars—or billions in today's currency. Before long the dirt streets were lined with saloons, stores, restaurants, banks, blacksmith shops, and livery stables, as well as homes and churches.

Silver and gold ore from the Comstock helped support the Northern cause during the Civil War and propelled Nevada toward statehood. Today Virginia City is a small but popular tourist town, allowing visitors to catch the flavor of an earlier era with board sidewalks, historic buildings, museums, a steam engine train, and tours of some of the old mines—where all the excitement began.

Over 150 years ago, thousands endured great hardships and risked their very lives to obtain precious metals from western America's streams and hills. All the while, however, there was great wealth much closer at hand. The Bible declares the priceless value of knowing and understanding God's Word. Job declared: "I have treasured the words of His mouth more than my necessary food" (Job 23:12 NKJV). David wrote: "The words of the LORD are flawless, like silver purified in a crucible, like gold refined seven times" (Psalm 42:6). God's wisdom is valuable because there's nothing like it in all the world. God understands our past, knows our future, and observes every detail of our lives. What's more, God is good. He loves us and desires our best. When He speaks to us through His Word and through His Spirit, His warnings, counsel, and encouragement are tailor-made for every situation we will ever face in life. You can't buy advice like this at any price. But if you come to God with a humble, receptive heart, you can obtain it free of charge.

Father, there is no wisdom anywhere like Yours. Keep me from careless steps and foolish choices today, and point me toward the best path. Your counsel is pure gold.

THE BEST CONSULTANT OF ALL KNOWS EVERY DETAIL OF YOUR LIFE—INCLUDING YOUR FUTURE.

San Diego Zoo
San Diego, California

THE CREATOR OF VARIETY

God spoke: "Earth, generate life! Every sort and kind:
cattle and reptiles and wild animals—all kinds."
And there it was:
wild animals of every kind,
Cattle of all kinds, every sort of reptile and bug.
God saw that it was good.

—GENESIS 1:24–25 MSG

For nearly one hundred years, the San Diego Zoo has been showcasing a wide, wonderful diversity of animal life in an eye-pleasing setting with an inviting sunny climate. Within its one hundred-acre expanse in historic Balboa Park, the zoo boasts a collection of more than four thousand animals representing more than eight hundred species from across the globe. The zoo has become known for its use of "cageless exhibits" and features many open-air attractions. The giant panda exhibit—one of only four in the world—has proved to be a very big draw since it opened in 1996. The lovable, endangered giants live with other companionable species in a large "bamboo forest" habitat. In just a few hours at San Diego's iconic zoo, you can see a Noah's-ark-variety of exotic, fearsome, entertaining residents of God's creation.

Although we humans live in a world of such endless variety, our own lives don't always reflect diversity. Many of us find security by sticking to established, familiar routines, preferences, patterns, habits, and practices. We have difficulty seeing beyond our own expectations. But not God. From the very beginning of everything, He has seemed to delight in an infinite array of options and possibilities. He created the ladybug and the brontosaurus, the giraffe and the lobster, the towering sequoias and perfect desert flowers so tiny you have to get down on your stomach to see them. When we bring Him our needs, concerns, and requests in prayer, we should never try to box Him in with our expectations of how or when He will answer. Yes, we can trust Him to act in love, in harmony with His Word, and in accord with His character. Beyond that, we have no idea how He will accomplish His goals or our good. But we can trust Him to do both.

Father, thank You that when I have run out of ideas and options, You have limitless creativity and wisdom. I trust You to show me answers I would have never come up with in a hundred years.

★ ★ ★

THE CREATOR OF ALL WILL NEVER RUN SHORT OF CREATIVE SOLUTIONS.

Chimney Rock National Historic Site Nebraska

THE LANDMARK

Do not remove the ancient landmark
Which your fathers have set.

—PROVERBS 22:28 NKJV

Rising up out of the North Platte River Valley in western Nebraska, Chimney Rock practically defines the term *landmark*. Its peak rises 470 feet above the surrounding terrain and is visible from the east for many miles. Centuries ago, before being worn away by erosion and lightning strikes, the iconic sandstone spire reached even higher over the plains and became the most famous and highly anticipated of all natural formations along the overland routes to California, Oregon, and Utah.

In the early 1800s, Chimney Rock was a welcome signpost for trappers, fur traders, and rugged mountain men making their way through Pawnee and Arapaho Indian territory to the mountains of the West. When they saw the tip of the famous rock on the far horizon, they knew how far they had come and took courage. In years to come, as wagon trains rolled through, Chimney Rock signaled the end of one phase of the journey and reminded the travelers of mountains to come. Those on the journey carved their names and other messages in the soft base of the chimney, only to have those words fade away with erosion and the passing of time.

We too need prominent landmarks in our lives, to give us encouragement, warn us of challenges ahead, and keep us on the right course. The Word of God gives us these markers as we make our way through the sometimes-confusing maze of life in the twenty-first century.

A landmark must be permanent, and God promised that His Word will never change. Jesus said, "Heaven and earth will pass away, but my words will never pass away" (Matthew 24:35). Unlike the messages carved years ago on Chimney Rock, God's Word will not be diminished or eroded by the passing of time. A landmark also offers direction, and Scripture provides endless instruction and counsel. The Lord says, "I will instruct you and teach you in the way you should go; I will counsel you with my loving eye on you" (Psalm 32:8).

Lord God, I am so grateful for the warnings, promises, and practical counsel in Your Book. Help me to make time to read my Bible and think about what it says every day.

GOD HAS GIVEN US HIS WORD TO KEEP US FROM VEERING OFF COURSE.

Fort McHenry
Baltimore, Maryland

STAND YOUR GROUND

Therefore put on the full armor of God, so that when the day of evil comes, you may be able to stand your ground, and after you have done everything, to stand.

—EPHESIANS 6:13

*I*t began as a poem written by an American lawyer after witnessing a shocking attack on Baltimore Harbor. He later reflected, "It seemed as though mother earth had opened and was vomiting shot and shell in a sheet of fire and brimstone."

On a rainy September 13, 1814, British warships unleashed a furious storm of shells and rockets onto Fort McHenry. The aerial bombardment went on for twenty-five hours. History books would later record the attack as the Battle of Baltimore, one of the final battles of the War of 1812. Weeks earlier, the British had launched an assault on Washington, DC, setting fire to the Capitol, the Treasury, and even the president's house.

As darkness fell, the lawyer, held aboard a British warship in the harbor, witnessed a final barrage that literally turned the night sky red. At dawn the captive American, Francis Scott Key, fully expected to see the British Union Jack raised over the wreckage of Fort McHenry. Instead, he saw a tattered "star-spangled banner" still flying over the ramparts. Somehow, the Americans had prevailed. And Key's poem, later set to music, became our country's national anthem.

Fort McHenry stands to this day in Baltimore Harbor, and the very flag that Key saw "by the dawn's early light" is still on display.

The apostle Paul describes the Christian's struggle against sin and Satan as an epic military battle. And though the fighting may become intense and the bombardment goes on and on, Paul calls on believers to "stand your ground" through it all. In the book of James we read: "Resist the devil, and he will flee from you" (James 4:7). Peter encourages us to "resist him, standing firm in the faith" (1 Peter 5:9).

When the night is finally over, the smoke clears, and daylight floods in, you will still be standing.

Father, I need Your help to stand my ground today. Please keep me strong when I feel weak, lift my head when I feel overwhelmed, and help me not to cave in or retreat when the opposition is strong. I want to stand in Jesus Christ today.

THE BATTLE MAY BE INTENSE, BUT GOD WILL ENABLE YOU TO STAND YOUR GROUND.

Painted Desert Arizona

SEVERE BEAUTY

*"I took care of you during the wilderness hard times,
those years when you had nothing.
I took care of you, took care of all your needs,
gave you everything you needed."*

—HOSEA 13:5-6 MSG

As far back as the 1600s, Spanish explorers who ventured across this stark landscape in what would become northeast Arizona called it *"El Desierto Pintado"*–The Painted Desert. This is an area of badlands lying within the Navajo Nation, comprising 93,500 acres and stretching from the Grand Canyon into the Petrified Forest National Park. Once you visit the region, it's easy to see how it came by its name. (And especially at sunset!) The rocks, ridges, canyons, and buttes display a painter's sample book of colors, from cool grays and subtle lavenders to bright oranges, vivid reds, and hot pinks. According to geologists, volcanic eruptions, earthquakes, floods, and sunlight both created and revealed the display across a vast canvas of clay and sandstone.

When we find ourselves in the midst of a desert situation in life, our biggest thought is about survival. We ask ourselves, "How will I ever get through this?" The ground beneath our feet is rough and uneven, days are hot, nights are cold, and loneliness stalks our steps. This wilderness season may involve wrestling with grief, depression, a financial crisis, a medical worry, or a wounded relationship. Whatever the cause, life isn't as easy as it was, and happiness and peace always seem just out of reach. Eventually, however, most of us do emerge into a better, more hopeful season. And after we have gained a little perspective, we may look back at our desert—and be surprised. It has a beauty that we couldn't even see when we were in the midst of it. We see God's provision, His kindness, and His companionship where we hadn't seen it before. He was there all along. He was faithful every day. He sent unexpected blessings. He gave us comfort in the night. Seen through fresh eyes, the dreadful wilderness was really a painted desert.

Father, I know that You've been in those dry, desert times. Thank You for walking with me, showing me beauty where I never expected to find any.

★ ★ ★

DIFFICULT SEASONS ARE EASIER TO BEAR WHEN WE DRAW ATTENTION TO GOD'S FAITHFULNESS.

Chickasaw National Recreation Area Oklahoma

OASIS

"The LORD will guide you always;
he will satisfy your needs in a sun-scorched land. . . .
You will be like a well-watered garden,
like a spring whose waters never fail."

—ISAIAH 58:11

Summer months can be very hot on America's plains and prairies. For generations, however, Oklahomans and many others have found a cool, refreshing refuge in the Chickasaw National Recreation Area. The 9,988-acre park has been called an oasis on the Oklahoma prairie. Vacationers seek out the streams, natural springs, waterfalls, swimming holes, and lakes of this protected area in the southern part of the state. As popular as the area is now, it was even more prominent years ago. In 1902, US Senator Orville Platt introduced legislation to set aside the area as a park. It was later designated Platt National Park, and with the coming of railroads to the area, it became immensely popular. In 1914, the park had more tourist traffic than either Yellowstone or Yosemite. Although the national park designation has been changed, visitors are still drawn to the shaded streams, campgrounds, wooded hiking paths, and two large man-made lakes.

After a day or two in the Chickasaw National Recreation Area, swimmers, boaters, and campers return, refreshed, to the summer heat of their cities and towns. In today's scripture, the Lord promised Israel that if the people would seek Him out and obey His Word, He would satisfy their needs as in a sun-scorched land. In other words, He would greatly refresh them with His own presence and blessing. And they, in turn, would become a "well-watered garden," and "a spring whose waters never fail." Many of the people we rub shoulders with every day are weighed down with problems, disappointments, and worries and could use some refreshment. As David wrote in Psalm 4:6, "There are many who say, 'Who will show us any good?'" (NKJV). If we have been daily refreshing ourselves in God's Word and in God's presence, we can become like a small, shady oasis to people in our world. We can be calm, positive, friendly, and hopeful when everyone else is wilting and out of sorts.

Father, my own well is dry and empty unless You fill me. May Your Spirit within me be like an artesian spring for the refreshment of others.

A POSITIVE WORD AND A SMILE FROM THE HEART CAN BE A SMALL OASIS IN SOMEONE'S UNHAPPY DAY.

Jackson Hole, Wyoming

IN THE PRESENCE OF MAJESTY

Let us be thankful, and so worship God acceptably with reverence and awe.

—HEBREWS 12:28

When it comes to mountains, Jackson Hole, Wyoming, has an overabundance of riches. Located in a large valley in northwestern Wyoming near the Idaho border, the town is literally encompassed by mountains. To the west lie the incomparable Tetons. To the north, there's Grand Teton National Park, and Yellowstone beyond that. To the east and south are the craggy peaks of the Gros Ventre Wilderness. In fact, this beautiful valley is a year-round hub of outdoor recreational pursuits. The town itself, with its famed Elk Horn Gates welcoming guests to the town square, retains its Wild West roots. False-fronted buildings, wooden sidewalks, and in the summer, a nightly "shoot-out" add to the cowboy ambience.

What would it be like to live in such a place, in full view of the mighty Tetons? Visitors, of course, are awed by the wild, rugged beauty. But what if you lived and worked there every day? Would you still see the majesty, or would you get used to it? Obviously, you couldn't stand around staring at mountains all day, or you wouldn't get any work done! But every now and then, rounding a corner, you might look up and feel a little surge of awe. In the early morning light, or maybe at sunset, your glance might be caught by the sight of those jagged peaks and pause for a few seconds, absorbing a scene too beautiful to ignore.

It's the same way in our walk with God. He is a wondrous, majestic Creator. David wrote that what he wanted to do most in life was "to gaze on the beauty of the Lord" (Psalm 27:4). The psalmist declared, "You are radiant with light, more majestic than mountains rich with game" (Psalm 76:4). We can't spend life on our knees simply marveling at God's beauty. But every now and then we catch a glimpse of who God is, the greatness of His power, love, and grace, and we draw in our breath a little. Wherever we are, we live and work in the presence of majesty.

Father, how great You are! And yet You invite us to live so very close to You. Please help me to never take this incredible privilege for granted.

★ ★ ★

MIRACLES SEEN EVERY DAY ARE STILL MIRACLES.

Northern Lights Anchorage, Alaska

THE FATHER OF LIGHTS

You are dressed in a robe of light.
You stretch out the starry curtain of the heavens.

—PSALM 104:2 NLT

The technical name is *Aurora Borealis*, "dawn of the north." Scientists explain that the mysterious lights result from collisions between gaseous particles in the earth's atmosphere with charged particles from the sun's atmosphere. The result is an unforgettable sky-wide display of "undulating curtains of light that glow, dance, ripple, sway, fold and unfold then suddenly disappear, only to reform in a new shape minutes later."*

In Anchorage, the bright, dancing lights are best viewed in fall, winter, and spring. Colors commonly include a pale, yellowish green, although dedicated watchers are sometimes rewarded with shades of red, yellow, green, blue, and violet. You don't have to travel very far from downtown Anchorage to find a vista point. The best viewing times are on subzero moonless nights, approaching midnight.

We read in the Bible's creation account that God's very first command, before all worlds, before the stars, was, "Let there be light." God and light are linked. In fact, the New Testament tells us that "God is light; in him there is no darkness at all." Paul tells that He "lives in unapproachable light." The psalmist

---

*http://www.anchorage.net/articles/northern-lights-anchorage-alaska

says that He is "radiant with light" and that He "wraps himself in light as with a garment" (Genesis 1:3; 1 John 1:5; 1 Timothy 6:16; Psalm 76:4, 104:2).

And sometimes, as in the case of the Northern Lights shining over Anchorage, He seems to *play* with light. We serve a majestic Creator God, who knows how to bring forth radiant beauty in the deep darkness of a long Arctic night in the dead of winter. As James wrote, "Every good gift and every perfect gift is from above, and comes down from the Father of lights" (James 1:17 NKJV). If God can create a magnificent light show in the middle of a night in the far north, then He can certainly bring light, hope, and even beauty out of the darkest, coldest, and dreariest seasons of your life.

> *Father of Lights, I praise You for Your beauty and majesty. Every good gift is from You. You are the God who can bring surprises and unexpected, unlooked-for moments of joy into my routine.*

**THE DARKEST SKIES MAKE THE BEST
CANVAS FOR PAINTINGS OF LIGHT.**

Niagara Falls, New York

"THE GOD OF GLORY THUNDERS"

The voice of the LORD is over the waters;
The God of glory thunders;
The LORD is over many waters.
The voice of the LORD is powerful;
The voice of the LORD is full of majesty.

—PSALM 29:3–4 NKJV

Do you hear it first or feel it in your chest? The sound of Niagara Falls is like a peal of continuous thunder. When you're close to it, perhaps in the *Maid of the Mist* boat edging through clouds of spray, it sounds like the roar of an ocean turned sideways. Spanning the border of the United States and Canada, what's known as Niagara Falls is the collective name for three falls: American, Bridal, and Horseshoe. These falls span a massive distance of 3,600 feet. Four of the five Great Lakes drain into the Niagara River and plummet over the great falls toward Lake Huron, forcing a mind-boggling 3,160 tons of water surging over the rocky, 170-foot cliff *every second*. Taken together, these five lakes comprise almost one-fifth of the world's fresh water supply.

The Bible compares God's voice to the sound of rushing water. The psalmist declared, "Mightier than the thunder of the great waters, mightier than the breakers of the sea—the LORD on high is mighty" (Psalm 93:4). The prophet said, "His voice was like the sound of many waters" (Ezekiel 43:2 NKJV). And when John saw the resurrected Jesus in His glory, he described His voice "as the sound of many waters" (Revelation 1:15 NKJV).

Is standing next to Niagara Falls at ninety-five decibels like hearing the voice of God? The writers of Scripture used earthly comparisons—thunder; ocean roar; and rushing, churning water. God could still speak that way if He chose, but He also speaks today through His Word, the Bible, and communicates with His sons and daughters in the deep places of their spirit. Sometimes it's like a whisper, a strong impression, or a "nudge." Elijah described it as a "still small voice" (1 Kings 19:12 NKJV).

God speaks in majestic ways through His creation, but He also speaks intimately, privately, and lovingly to those who listen daily for His voice and long for His counsel.

Spirit of God, I do want to hear Your voice today. Help me to filter out the background noise and static as You speak words of life into my heart. My ears are open to hear You.

★ ★ ★

GOD SHOUTS THROUGH THE MIGHT OF HIS CREATION,
BUT SPEAKS QUIET WORDS OF LOVE TO HIS OWN.

Battleship Memorial Park Mobile, Alabama

READY FOR SERVICE

"So you also must be ready, because the Son of Man will come at an hour when you do not expect him."

—MATTHEW 24:44

It took sixteen months to build and launch her, but she was only in commission for less than five years. In that time, however, the *USS Alabama* fought in both the Atlantic and Pacific regions, from the Arctic Circle to the Fiji Islands, earning nine World War II battle stars. The *Alabama* had fired over 1,250 sixteen-inch shells on the enemy and shot down twenty-two enemy aircraft—but never was damaged by hostile forces and never lost a single man to enemy fire. At the war's end, she led the victorious US fleet into Tokyo Bay.

In the Battleship Memorial Park and Museum in Mobile, Alabama, visitors from all over the world have the opportunity to tour this restored battleship, a World War II submarine, and numerous other military displays. On board the *Alabama*, visitors can explore the ship's twelve decks, peer inside the impressive gun turrets, and try to get a feel for what life was like for the crew of 2,332 enlisted men and officers who called the ship home.

Even though the *USS Alabama* was decommissioned after sixty months, the ship had helped turn the tide of battle. The period of usefulness may have been brief, but it was strategic.

As followers of Jesus, we too have just one brief lifetime to make a difference for Him. As a result, it's important to be awake, alert, and ready to be used in strategic ways. The apostle Peter wrote: "Always be prepared to give an answer to everyone who asks you to give the reason for the hope that you have" (1 Peter 3:15). Paul told Timothy we need to be like an instrument or tool that God can pick up and use anytime—"useful to the Master and prepared to do any good work" (2 Timothy 2:21). When He gives us something to do or somewhere to be or something to say, we've got to be ready to respond.

Father, help me to be ready day by day for those moments when You give me a task and ask me to step forward in faith.

★ ★ ★

THE TOOLS THE LORD REACHES FOR ARE
WILLING, READY, AND AVAILABLE.

Glacier National Park
Montana

THE LAST, BEST PLACE

Now we live with great expectation, and we have a priceless
inheritance—an inheritance that is kept in heaven for you, pure
and undefiled, beyond the reach of change and decay.

—1 PETER 1:3-4 NLT

Montana's official state motto is *"Oro y Plata,"* which is Spanish for "gold and silver." One of the state's unofficial mottos, however, has more emotional impact: "The last, best place." And up in the northwest corner of the state, the crown jewel of Montana—and perhaps all of America—is Glacier National Park. Those who have toured Glacier and sit down to write about it run out of adjectives. *Magnificent. Epic. Untamed. Awe-inspiring.* It's difficult to wrap words around a million acres of towering, majestic mountains; steep, glacier-carved valleys; seven hundred miles of trails; and 762 blue lakes, shimmering under that big Montana sky. Glacier is unique in that almost all of its original plant and animal life has been preserved. Mountain goats, moose, wolverines, grizzly bears, and scores of other species still roam through the park. In other words, it is one place in the continental United States that has remained pristine and unspoiled. The apostle Peter wrote to Christians of a pure and undefiled inheritance. He assured those who had been persecuted and scattered that even if they lose homes and possessions, they have a home in heaven, a priceless inheritance being kept for them.

What's more, this future residence is "beyond the reach of change and decay."

We live in a world that's constantly moving and changing all around us. And not always for the better! Carole King's popular song from the 1970s asked the question, "Doesn't anybody stay in one place anymore?" Just about everything in our experience here on earth shifts and alters as the years go by—houses, neighborhoods, friendships, careers, and perhaps even our health. How encouraging to remember that no matter what, we have a home in heaven that will *never* change, age, fade, or lose value in any way—and with a God who is the same yesterday, today, and tomorrow.

Father, thank You that I don't have to fear changes, disruptions, and setbacks in this life because You have already reserved a place in heaven for me, ready for the day and hour of my arrival.

★ ★ ★

THE TRUE LAST, BEST PLACE IS WHEREVER
JESUS WAITS FOR ME.

Golden Gate Bridge
San Francisco, California

BRIDGING THE GAP

You were lost, without God, without hope. But now you belong to Christ Jesus,
and though you once were far away from God, now you have been brought very
near to him because of what Jesus Christ has done for you with his blood.

—EPHESIANS 2:12–13 TLB

It became known as "the bridge that couldn't be built." Far-sighted planners and engineers had dreamed for decades about a bridge that would span the Golden Gate Strait, the channel linking San Francisco Bay to the Pacific Ocean. Beautiful as San Francisco might have been, it was isolated by its geography and dependent on ferry boats for its livelihood. Those who dreamed of a bridge linking the San Francisco peninsula with Marin County, however, were opposed by a host of experts who claimed it couldn't be done. The 6,700-foot strait was too wide and too deep. Currents and tides were too strong, and when you considered the sudden, blustery winds and the thick blankets of fog, the whole idea was too dangerous, too costly, and virtually unfeasible.

After decades of debate, however, the project was launched on January 5, 1933, and completed four years later on May 28, 1937. Today the graceful orange span is one of America's most familiar and beloved landmarks.

The Bible makes it clear that the relationship bridge between God and man has been completely shattered by sin. The Bible says, "Your iniquities have separated you from your God; your sins have hidden his face from you, so that he will not hear" (Isaiah 59:2). Paul wrote, "You lived in this world without God and without hope" (Ephesians 2:12 NLT). The gap between a holy God and sinful men and women was too wide, too far, too deep. From all appearances, it was the bridge that couldn't be built. How could God ever span such a gap?

Jesus, the Son of God, became the bridge Himself. On the cross, He gave His own life to save humans from eternal separation from God. Jesus Christ is the bridge to eternal life.

Father, in a million years I could never have found a way to reach You, to bridge the terrible distance between us. But You did what I could never do for myself. You sent Your Son Jesus to be a bridge between earth and heaven.

★ ★ ★

ONLY A GOD OF UNLIMITED LOVE AND UNLIMITED POWER COULD BRIDGE AN IMPOSSIBLE DISTANCE.

North Dakota

A SPACIOUS PLACE

When hard pressed, I cried to the LORD;
he brought me into a spacious place.

—PSALM 118:5

With a landmass of 70,762 square miles, North Dakota is a large, mostly flat state in the Upper Midwest with abundant grassland and massive room to sprawl. It is the third least-populated state in America and has the fewest visitors. But it also has a wide variety of wildlife, rich natural resources, a wide unobstructed horizon, and the lowest crime rates and unemployment in the nation. In North Dakota, the American buffalo still roam the prairies. So do bighorn sheep, deer, elk, moose, and pronghorns. The state's human population has remained essentially the same for years—and isn't significantly higher than it was one hundred years ago. A recent oil and natural gas boom made possible by new drilling technologies has brought jobs and prosperity to North Dakota. Even so, visitors will find mile upon mile of uncluttered roads and trails, ample peace and quiet, and plentiful outdoor activities including hunting, fishing, camping, boating, bird-watching, and cross-country skiing.

Less than a tenth the size of North Dakota, the land of Israel was never a very big place. But when David was running for his life from King Saul and his army, it seemed smaller than ever. Everywhere the young fugitive turned, someone would recognize him and give him away. But then David cried out to God and found a spacious place where he could breathe easily for a while. Was it a literal piece of land somewhere beyond Saul's reach? Perhaps, but more likely it was a rest and peace of soul that God brought to David right in the middle of his distress. The fact is, most of us know how it feels to be pressed in by circumstances, deadlines, job pressures, or health concerns. Like the apostle Paul, we could say, "We are hard pressed on every side" (2 Corinthians 4:8). But even when we're up to our ears in the pressures of life, there is a refuge in God's sheltering hands where we can find rest—and room to breathe. As Paul wrote, "For he himself is our peace" (Ephesians 2:14).

Father God, when I am squeezed by pressures, You are the One who guides my feet to a spacious place.

THE BREATHING SPACE WE SEEK IS IN A PERSON,
NOT A PLANE TICKET OR TRAVEL BROCHURE.

San Juan Islands
Puget Sound, Washington

VITAL CONNECTIONS

May the God who gives endurance and encouragement give you the same attitude of mind toward each other that Christ Jesus had.

—ROMANS 15:5

The San Juan Islands, scattered throughout the Puget Sound in the northwest corner of the United States, belong to the state of Washington. There are over 400 islands (with only 128 named), and they are located between the United States mainland and Canada's Vancouver Island. Collectively, the islands have over 478 miles of shoreline. Since there are no bridges from island to island, residents and visitors alike must rely on air travel, boats, or the state ferry system, which connects the mainland with the four largest islands: Lopez, Shaw, Orcas, and San Juan. The islands are a major tourist destination, with hiking, biking, scuba diving, and orca whale-watching included in the favorite activities. With many options for restaurants and accommodations on the main islands, and a drier, warmer climate than nearby Seattle, the islands entice visitors to spend a day, a week, or a summer exploring the many beaches and trails and soaking in a more leisurely pace of life.

John Donne, a seventeenth-century English poet, once wrote, "No man is an island, entire of itself, every man is a piece of the continent, a part of the main." However else that bit of verse might apply to today's world, it is certainly true of the church of Jesus Christ. The New Testament letters tie believers together with numerous exhortations. In Hebrews, the author warned stay-at-home believers to "not neglect our meeting together, as some people do, but encourage one another" (10:25 NLT). Jesus said, "Love one another." The apostle Paul returned to the theme time and again: Be devoted to one another. . . . Live in harmony with one another. . . . Accept one another. . . . Instruct one another. . . . Greet one another. . . . Serve one another. . . . Bear with one another. . . . Forgive one another.* As a missionary-pastor, Paul's heart was concerned that believers be making vital connections with one another and that their lives be tied together with lifelines of love, compassion, loyalty, and selfless service.

Lord, help me to reach out beyond myself today, making a call, sending an e-mail, writing a note, or inviting someone to lunch. Help me to be less preoccupied with my own needs and more in tune with the needs of my brothers and sisters.

ISOLATION HAS NO PLACE IN THE FAMILY OF JESUS CHRIST.

* *John 13:34; Romans 12:10, 16; 15:7, 14; 16:16; Galatians 5:13; Ephesians 4:2, 32*

Statue of Liberty National Monument New York Harbor

A SYMBOL . . . AND MORE

As for me, God forbid that I should boast about anything
except the cross of our Lord Jesus Christ.

—GALATIANS 6:14 TLB

A gift like no other, it has become the ultimate symbol around the world for freedom and democracy. Erected in New York Harbor and dedicated in October 1886, the Statue of Liberty was a gift of friendship from the people of France. For millions of immigrants drawing near to New York City after long ocean voyages, Lady Liberty was one of the first glimpses of America. On the day she was dedicated, the tricolor French flag veiled her face. In a dramatic flourish, the designer and sculptor himself climbed the 354 steps within his own creation to release the flag and unveil the noble, now-familiar face. The statue is 151 feet high, from base to torch—354 feet with pedestal and foundation included. The seven points on her crown represent the seven seas and the seven continents of the world. In other words, Liberty is a universal yearning, not just a national symbol.

At the turn of the twentieth century, the great structure fell under the jurisdiction of the United States Lighthouse Board because the Lady's illuminated torch served as a navigational aid for ships entering the harbor. The statue became, then, a symbol and something much more.

It is the same with the cross of Jesus Christ. Across the world, it is an easily recognizable symbol of Christianity. In reality, however, it is a real and powerful navigational tool that has guided untold millions out of darkness, superstition, selfishness, addiction, and despair, bringing them into relationship with their Creator. To those who live apart from Christ, the cross is a religious icon or decorative emblem. But for those who have experienced its mighty transformational power, the cross is more like a shining torch lifted high on a dark night, welcoming them to safety.

Lord Jesus, thank You for the cross. If it wasn't for that place and time in history where You laid down Your life for me, I would have no hope at all. But now I have every hope—of meaningful life today and a future in heaven.

THE CROSS MARKS THE PLACE IN TIME AND SPACE WHEN HUMANITY WAS TRULY SET FREE.

Nashville, Tennessee

A NEW SONG

He put a new song in my mouth,
a hymn of praise to our God.

—PSALM 40:3

The last Greyhound from Muncie rolls into the Nashville station amidst the final traces of sunset. A young man wearing cowboy boots emerges with a backpack and guitar, and eagerly steps into a hot and humid Tennessee night. In his backpack, he carries a dozen copies of a CD cut with his best songs to be handed to "the right people." It really doesn't seem like much of a plan, but it's worked for other country singers, so why not take a chance?

Nashville has a million stories of its own, and that's as it should be. Because country music is all about true life stories. Heartfelt ballads, accompanied by guitars, banjos, or fiddles, set feet in motion and pluck at the heartstrings. From the mid-1950s into the 1960s, Nashville, Tennessee, became the center of a multimillion dollar country music industry. From that time it was Johnny Cash, Patsy Cline, and Hank Williams on the radio or TV; today residents are accustomed to seeing modern country stars anywhere from eating at a local pancake house to playing in sold-out auditoriums. Many popular tourist sites in this beautiful city on the Cumberland River involve country music. These include the Country Music Hall of Fame and Museum, Belcourt Theatre, and Ryman Auditorium, the original home of the Grand Ole Opry.

Country music represents a huge slice of American culture and experience. While the lyrics and melodies express a full spectrum of emotions, they often speak of our disappointment and sadness. We're heartbroken when people we love and trust prove false, fickle, or untrue. We're wounded by lies and betrayals. In a sense, these are the "old songs" of humanity, going back to the beginning of time. But when we turn to God, really take hold of His promises, and experience His personal presence, we find that we have a new song. With our sins washed away in Christ, we find a reason for living, and deep-down peace. We want to sing something new, rather than the same old sad songs everyone else is singing. God gives us a fresh confidence, a light heart, and a song created just for us—to sing back to Him.

Father God, fill my heart and my mouth with a fresh song of hope and confidence today. May my life show a contrast to the sad, disappointed, and sometimes bitter music all around me.

NEW SONGS CAN BE LIVED AS WELL AS SUNG. HOPE MAKES ITS OWN MUSIC.

The Grand Canyon
Arizona

TOO WIDE TO JUMP

*It was through what his Son did that God cleared a path for everything
to come to him—all things in heaven and on earth—for Christ's death
on the cross has made peace with God for all by his blood.*

—COLOSSIANS 1:20 TLB

"The Grand Canyon fills me with awe," wrote Theodore Roosevelt. "It is beyond comparison—beyond description; absolutely unparalleled throughout the wide world." Roosevelt's admiration, however, went far beyond words. As president in 1908, he founded what was called the Grand Canyon National Monument; eleven years later, this Arizona treasure became a national park. Anyone standing on the rim looking into the mile-deep chasm—or at the opposite rim, up to 18 miles away—experiences a sense of their own smallness. The canyon extends for 277 miles, and the park itself covers over 1.2 million acres. Seeing the canyon at sunset with its layered, serrated cliffs flaming with color is a lifelong memory. Those who make the long trek down into the canyon face a difficult, potentially dangerous hike, but also experience sights and secrets that can't be seen from the rim.

There is no bridge across the Grand Canyon, and those who want to travel from rim-to-rim must do so on foot or take the long drive around. No one thinks of crossing the canyon with a jump. It's impossible. Unthinkable. The distance is much too great and human abilities are much too small. In the same way, no one can reach a holy God or enter His heaven by self-effort—no matter how sincere that attempt might be. It can't be done. It would be like trying to jump across the Grand Canyon. Isaiah 59:2 says, "Your iniquities have separated you from your God; your sins have hidden his face from you, so that he will not hear." Romans 3:23 says, "For all have sinned and fall short of the glory of God." It would take a mighty bridge to span the great gulf between God and sinful human beings. And that bridge was the cross of Jesus Christ, God's Son, who gave Himself for our sins.

Father, I'm so grateful for Jesus and His cross. Without Him, I would have no hope of knowing You and no hope of heaven. Thank You, Father, for bridging that canyon for me.

★ ★ ★

EVERY GLIMPSE OF THE GRAND CANYON SHOULD REMIND US OF A GREATER CANYON AND A CROSS-SHAPED BRIDGE.

Maui, Hawaii

MEDITATION IN THE SAND

How precious are your thoughts about me, O God.
They cannot be numbered!
I can't even count them;
they outnumber the grains of sand!

—PSALM 139:17-18 NLT

To longtime residents of Maui, another morning is just that—a day to pursue work, responsibilities, and a thousand other everyday concerns. But for a visitor in Maui on a short stay, each day is a treasure—something to be savored slowly and tucked away in memory. And if you've never visited, you might as well release your cynicism, because it truly is as delightful as everyone says it is.

Maui is the second largest of the Hawaiian Islands and a favored destination for nature lovers, shoppers, hikers, snorkelers, whale-watchers, and those who simply want to soak up sunlight on a beach surrounded by palm trees and tropical flowers. Evening, when soft trade winds rustle the palm trees, is a perfect time to stroll the streets of historic Lahaina on the island's west side, with a variety of shops, galleries, and restaurants. At sunset, most everyone stops what they're doing to look out across the Pacific and watch the colors wash across sky and ocean alike.

While you are seated on the warm sand at Kaanapali Beach, looking out across the ocean toward the island of Molokai, cup your hand for a moment and scoop up a handful of sand. How many grains of sand are there in that scoop? Can you count them? Could you count the grains of sand in one teaspoon? In a quarter teaspoon? David wrote that God's thoughts toward each one of us outnumber the grains of sand *in the whole world.* This is something we need to remember when we feel alone, uncared for, unappreciated, or forgotten. We might even feel disregarded by God or wonder if He has misplaced our file on His desk. It isn't true. At this very moment, you are on God's mind and in His thoughts. If you responded to Him in this moment, He could accurately reply, "I was just thinking about you!"

> *Father, I believe Your Word when You say that You think about me constantly, but sometimes the truth doesn't penetrate my loneliness, my discouragement. Let the reality of Your concern and care warm my heart today.*

★ ★ ★

**GOD DOESN'T NEED TO PENCIL ME IN TO HIS CALENDAR.
MY NAME IS WRITTEN ON THE PALM OF HIS HAND.**

Iowa State Fair
Des Moines, Iowa

WHEN THE FAMILY GATHERS

Let us think of ways to motivate one another to acts of love and good works.
And let us not neglect our meeting together, as some people do, but encourage
one another, especially now that the day of his return is drawing near.

HEBREWS 10:24-25 NLT

Every year the state of Iowa hosts a family get-together on a *very* large scale. Spread out over 450 acres, the Iowa State Fair draws over a million visitors annually to Des Moines. It's been called "Iowa's great celebration," "America's classic state fair," and "the true heartbeat of the American Midwest." For generations, the big fair has been an opportunity for Iowa families to work together on showing their prized animals, produce, and crafts. It's also a chance for young and old alike to stroll through the manicured grounds, take a ride on the ten-acre midway, watch a live concert in the grandstands, or maybe just walk around munching on an elephant ear or corn dog—or some other treat from one of the two hundred food stands. In short, it's a place for being together and making memories.

Shared memories belong to those who deliberately step out of their isolation and link up with others to do something together. In today's world, much of this closeness has been replaced by our electronic devices. Everywhere you look, you see people with their smartphones or tablets, tapping away on their screens and seemingly in a world of their own. Yet in spite of all this high-tech communication, people today seem more lonely and isolated than ever. It's easier to stay home than get together with others. Easier to do FaceTime than invite someone over. Easier to text someone far away than speak to someone two feet away.

Christ wants His people to reach out to one another, encourage one another, and comfort one another. That's why there are so many "one another" verses in the New Testament! God's family needs to spend time together—for worship and teaching, but also for dinners, movies, games, walks, and helping neighbors. Psalm 68:6 says that "God sets the lonely in families," or put another way, "makes homes for the homeless" (MSG), but He expects His people to do the inviting.

Lord Jesus, forgive me for my tendency to shut others out of my life. I pray this day for an opportunity to encourage someone, lend a hand to someone, or somehow to brighten someone's day and to do it in Your strength and in Your name.

NO MATTER HOW BUSY OR PRESSURED HIS DAY, JESUS ALWAYS SAW PEOPLE IN HIS PERIPHERAL VISION.

Jersey Shore New Jersey

THE GOD WHO RESTORES

Finally, brothers and sisters, rejoice! Strive for full restoration, encourage one another, be of one mind, live in peace.

—2 CORINTHIANS 13:11

For generations, the Jersey Shore—a 127-mile length of the New Jersey coastline—has been a place where families have returned summer after summer. From Sandy Hook in the north to Cape May in the south, "the Shore" offers community after community and beach after beach for vacationers and retirees looking for fun and relaxation. For nearly a hundred years, tourists have been attracted to the area's beaches, amusement parks, boardwalks, restaurants, and hotels.

Early on October 29, 2012, Hurricane Sandy made landfall just northeast of Atlantic City, ravaging much of America's Eastern Seaboard. Sandy was the largest Atlantic hurricane on record and became the second-costliest storm in US history. It was especially devastating to the Jersey Shore, flooding towns, ripping up boardwalks, dumping homes and hotels off foundations, and tearing away sandy beaches. Since those devastating days, however, federal, state, and private efforts have restored many businesses, homes, and recreational areas. New piers and boardwalks have replaced historic structures, and old, familiar food shops, candy stores, and bakeries have reopened. The Jersey Shore never will be quite the same because so much was washed away, but families can return again, summer by summer, resuming old traditions or beginning new ones.

The God we serve is a God of restoration. At the end of the ages He will restore all things (Acts 3:21). But until then, He is Lord over countless, smaller restorations. He restores individual lives . . . marriages . . . families . . . friend-ships . . . health . . . trust . . . finances . . . careers. Through it all, He renews peace, happiness, and a strong sense of purpose. The psalmist wrote: "Though you have made me see troubles, many and bitter, you will restore my life again . . . and comfort me once more" (Psalm 71:20–21). Sin and selfishness destroy much in this life, and full restoration won't happen until heaven. But in the meantime, God's power and grace may reconstruct much of what has been lost, blighted, or frittered away. What's more, He will create brand-new hopes, dreams, and opportunities for the sake of His kingdom.

Praise You, Father, that You are a God who restores, rebuilds, redeems, and renews.

WHEN I PUT ALL THE BROKEN PIECES OF LIFE IN YOUR HANDS, YOU CREATE SOMETHING NEW.

National World War II Museum New Orleans, Louisiana

EVENTS THAT SHAPED THE WORLD

*The gospel is bearing fruit and growing throughout the
whole world—just as it has been doing among you since the
day you heard it and truly understood God's grace.*

—COLOSSIANS 1:6

The National World War II Museum opened its doors in 2000 and quickly became one of New Orleans' top attractions. The museum's exhibits cover the massive scope of the war without ignoring the personal stories of individual lives touched by the conflict. While D-Day and the Battle of Normandy were the museum's original emphasis, the exhibits also provide perspective on the war in the Pacific, where the Allies fought Japan island-to-island and eventually unleashed a nuclear nightmare over Hiroshima and Nagasaki. Visitors should plan on spending up to three hours viewing the interactive exhibits, leaving time to take in the 4-D award winning film *Beyond All Boundaries*, produced and narrated by Tom Hanks.

America's involvement in World War II was just a little under four years. If you've ever spoken to anyone who lived through those events, those few years still loom very large. Yes, they were years that shaped the globe, but they also shaped untold millions of individual lives. The suffering was so great, the battles so fierce, the defeats so terrible, and the triumphs so earth-shaking that virtually every person on the planet must have been touched in some way.

The Lord Jesus' ministry on earth was around three-and-a-half years. And during that time, that one life changed the world for all time, impacting eternity. The effect of His coming was so profound that humankind started its calendar over again, dating everything from His birth, death, and resurrection. Jesus not only shaped past history, but He also continues to this moment to shape lives. His blood still covers the greatest sins. His power and wisdom can change the whole course of a life. *Any* life, *any*where, *any*time.

Lord Jesus, I believe that You are able to change my destiny and the very direction of my life, beginning today.

**THE ONE WHO CHANGED EARTH'S HISTORY HAS
NO DIFFICULTY CHANGING MY HISTORY.**

Pikes Peak
Colorado

THE HIGH VIEW

"Be sure to fear the LORD and serve him faithfully with all your heart; consider what great things he has done for you."

—1 SAMUEL 12:24–25

We stood at last on that Gate-of-Heaven summit . . . and gazed in wordless rapture over the far expanse of mountain ranges and the sea-like sweep of plain." So wrote Katharine Lee Bates, an English teacher from Massachusetts, in her diary after her first visit to the summit of Pikes Peak in 1893. Later, still awed by her experience, she wrote a poem that became one of our country's great anthems—*America, the Beautiful*.

Pike's Peak has that effect on people. It's the second most-visited mountain in the world (after Fuji) and has been called "America's Mountain." Katharine Bates made her summit journey by carriage and the last six miles by mule. Today you can drive to the top, ride on the Pikes Peak Cog Railway, or hike Barr Trail. The 14,115-foot summit is open year-round, depending on weather conditions. From the top you can still fill your eyes with "purple mountain majesties" and "the fruited plain," as well as the city of Colorado Springs far below.

But most of us don't take time for a long view of life; we're too busy living it. Wrapped up in the many details of work, family, school, and personal pursuits, we don't think much about our lives as a whole. As a result, it doesn't occur to us to reflect on all that God has done for us. We lose any sense of wonder over

His kindness, protection, mercy, miraculous provision, healing, and guidance. That's why we need to pull back at times and try for a wider, higher view. How quickly we forget how many times He has forgiven us, rescued us from empty self-centeredness, lifted us out of swamps, healed our self-inflicted wounds, and met us at major crossroads, pointing us in the right direction. That's why we need Pikes Peak moments in our lives, when we take time to look back, look ahead, and give God thanks.

Lord, I look back and just marvel. I praise You for years of protection, provision, counsel, and songs in the night. Help me to remember all You have done and to give You the praise You deserve.

★ ★ ★

THE FAITHFUL ONE WHO BROUGHT YOU THIS FAR WILL STAY WITH YOU FOR THE WHOLE JOURNEY.

White Sands
New Mexico

CHANGING THE CHARACTER OF DARKNESS

"He reveals the deep things of darkness
and brings utter darkness into the light."

—JOB 12:22

If you have ever wondered what it might look like to visit another planet in our galaxy, you might experience something very similar in a setting much closer to home, without the hassle of a bulky space suit. The White Sands National Monument near the southern border of New Mexico is like no place else in America—or possibly on earth. The "sands" are really white gypsum crystals, and the monument consists of 275 square miles of shifting, moving, snow-white dunes—the largest such dune field in the world.

For the adventurous, there are hikes through this other-worldly landscape. Some families bring along plastic sleds for downhill dune sledding. One of the unique characteristics of gypsum is that it doesn't absorb heat. As a result, you can comfortably walk barefoot across the sand on the hottest summer day. Some say that moonlit nights are the best, when the dunes seem to glow with a light of their own. Even the darkest of nights, far from city lights, doesn't seem that dark in a wilderness of cool white sand.

In a moment of awe and wonder, David once wrote, "My God turns my darkness into light" (Psalm 18:28). Did that mean that David no longer experienced dark nights, dark moments, or dark situations? No. But somehow the very nature of that darkness had been changed. With God by his side, darkness just wasn't as dark. In Psalm 139:11, he wrote: "If I try to hide in the darkness, the night becomes light around me" (TLB). Everyone, including followers of Christ, must experience some of the darkness of this dark world. Like everyone else, our lives will be touched by illness, disappointment, loss, and death. Jesus said, "In this world you will have trouble. But take heart! I have overcome the world" (John 16:33).

Even in very dark moments, God's truth and God's presence in our lives will glow, and to the wondering eyes of others, so will we.

Thank You, Father, that You are always with me, day and night. Even in the darkest, dreariest hours, You light the situation from within, giving me perspective, comfort, and hope.

THE LIGHT OF GOD'S PRESENCE CHANGES THE CHARACTER OF THE DARKNESS.

Wheat Fields of Kansas

HARVEST

"Don't you have a saying, 'It's still four months until harvest'? I tell you, open your eyes and look at the fields! They are ripe for harvest."

—JOHN 4:35

When you think of Kansas, images of Dorothy, tornadoes, ruby slippers, and the Land of Oz might come to mind. But in reality, Kansas is all about wheat. It is the largest wheat-producing state in America and has been called "the bread basket of the world." Located in the very heart of the country, Kansas grows enough wheat each year to produce thirty-six billion loaves of bread. Planted in September, the green wheat grows to a height of two to four feet, and by early summer, begins to change color. At harvest in June and July, the wheat has ripened into a rich golden hue. When the wheat heads become heavy with grain and begin to nod in the wind, the farmer knows that harvest-time is near. Watching the wide fields of wheat ripple and toss like waves under a deep blue Kansas sky is one of the richest, most peaceful experiences in all fifty states.

In John 4, Jesus used the analogy of grain fields and an upcoming harvest. When Jesus and the twelve disciples stopped for lunch in Sychar, Samaria, no doubt they thought of it as a wide spot in the road between Judea and Galilee. In their minds, they were simply passing through. Back up in Galilee, they may have reasoned, they could get involved in some serious ministry. But Jesus said, "Open your eyes. Look at what's right in front of you!" He was talking about the people in that village who had heard a report about Jesus and wanted to see

Him for themselves. It's a good reminder for every believer. In the course of our day, we will meet people who have been edging toward faith for a long time and might turn to Jesus with a little encouragement. The Lord is saying here, "Be aware. Keep your eyes and ears open. Let My Spirit lead you to people who are seeking Me at this very moment!"

Lord, sometimes I'm too occupied with myself to be thinking about a potential harvest all around me. Please open my eyes to people who are already reaching out to You.

★ ★ ★

BEGIN EACH DAY BY ASKING THE LORD, "WHO IS READY?"

Bar Harbor, Maine

LIGHT KEEPERS

"No one lights a lamp and hides it in a clay jar or puts it under a bed. Instead,
they put it on a stand, so that those who come in can see the light."

—LUKE 8:16

*B*ar Harbor, on Frenchman Bay in Maine, has been a national treasure on American's northeast Atlantic coast for generations. Years ago, this small coastal community on Mount Desert Island became a fashionable retreat for wealthy families seeking to escape the hubbub of city life. Some stately mansions and grand old hotels still remind visitors of Bar Harbor's lavish, high-society past, but life dramatically changed when a devastating 1947 wildfire swept through the town. In a little less than three hours, the fire razed 170 homes, scores of cottages, and five large, historic hotels.

Today the restored town is filled with visitors drawn by the scenery, the shops, the seafood—including the famous, succulent lobster rolls—the many hotels and inns, and abundant outdoor activities in the adjoining Acadia National Park. One of the more popular attractions is a lighthouse boat tour along the majestic coastline, giving visitors an up-close look at the area's five historic lighthouses. The grandfather among them, Baker Island Light, was warning sailing ships away from the rocks as early as 1828.

The image of a lighthouse—its bright beam cutting through darkness and fog—has always been a compelling metaphor of the Christian life. Solomon wrote, "Light in a messenger's eyes brings joy to the heart, and good news gives health to the bones" (Proverbs 15:30). The Lord Jesus has called us to be messengers with light in our eyes. Because we have experienced forgiveness of sin, companionship with God, and the hope of heaven when we die, followers of Christ ought to be the most joyful, *light*-hearted men and women in all the world. Messengers with light in their eyes are those with encouraging news they can't wait to tell others. The world we occupy today has all the disappointment, cynicism, and negativity it can bear. What people need to see (whether they realize it or not) is a messenger filled with light.

Lord Jesus, I pray that Your presence would be so real in me today that I would somehow bring hope and light into every room I enter.

★ ★ ★

TODAY'S WORLD DOESN'T NEED MORE PROPHETS OF GLOOM. BUT THERE'S ALWAYS ROOM FOR ANOTHER LIGHTHOUSE.

Washington Monument
Washington, DC

COUNT THE COST

"Suppose one of you wants to build a tower. Won't you first sit down and estimate the cost to see if you have enough money to complete it? For if you lay the foundation and are not able to finish it, everyone who sees it will ridicule you."

—LUKE 14:28-29

*W*hen the United States decided to honor the father of the country with a monument, it was with feelings of profound gratitude and respect. Who, after all, had been more indispensable to the nation's founding? Whether as military commander of the Continental Army or as the first president, George Washington set a high standard for all who would follow. The ambitious monument bearing his name, however, had difficulties from the start. Construction began in 1848, but the project experienced a serious funding shortfall—and then bankruptcy. There were political battles, congressional squabbles, and hostile power-grabs by opposing factions. And then came the Civil War, when progress halted altogether. The partially finished monument, at a height of 150 feet, stood like a pathetic broken stub for twenty-three years. Construction finally resumed in 1877, and was completed in 1884. When the aluminum cap was placed on the top, the marble monument was the highest building in the world, at 555 feet. The words inscribed on the cap read: *"Laus Deo"* (Praise be to God).

When Jesus told the story about some builders who left a tower half finished, He really wasn't talking about construction projects or monuments; He was speaking about people's lives. Large crowds had been following Him, but Jesus knew that most of these people were only looking for a little excitement and diversion in their lives—they never really intended to become disciples. It can be the same with us. We might make a show of surrendering our lives to Jesus, but when it comes to some hard decisions about our personal lives or lifestyles, we may not be ready to follow through or put Him first. The Lord Himself said, "Anyone who wants to follow me must put aside his own desires and conveniences and carry his cross with him every day and keep close to me!" (Luke 9:23 TLB).

Lord, I look to You today for the grace and courage to follow through with the person You have called me to be and what You have called me to do.

DON'T LET YOUR WORDS RUN AHEAD OF A
TRUE COMMITMENT FROM THE HEART.

The Bluebonnets of Texas

A REMINDER OF HIS CARE

*"Think of the wild flowers, and how they neither work nor weave. Yet I tell
you that Solomon in all his glory was never arrayed like one of these."*

—LUKE 12:27 PHILLIPS

Texas historian Jack Maguire once observed and is quoted often, "The blue-bonnet is to Texas what the shamrock is to Ireland, the cherry blossom to Japan, the lily to France, the rose to England, and the tulip to Holland."

In a state known for wide horizons, towering ambitions, big hats, and tall tales, this humble little wildflower holds a large place in every heart. For two months in early spring, hayfields, pastures, hillsides, and prairie landscapes reaching to the edge of vision are awash with indigo blooms. Maguire went on to say that the bluebonnet was "not only the state flower but also a kind of floral trademark almost as well known to outsiders as cowboy boots and the Stetson hat." While New Englanders talk about fall foliage and Georgians celebrate their elegant dogwoods, Texans take fierce pride in the sea of blue that washes up against their cities and towns and covers their vast grasslands. The two predominant species of bluebonnets grow naturally in Texas and nowhere else in the world. While the "yellow rose of Texas" may have a refined, cultivated beauty, it's this tiny ground flower with bonnet-shaped petals that inspires the most loyalty in the Lone Star State . . . and draws admirers from across the nation.

When Jesus walked on this earth, He drew attention to the wildflowers of Israel. He said, "Consider the lilies of the field, how they grow" (Matthew 6:28 NKJV). As He spoke, He looked out across the crowds of people who came to hear Him, so troubled and weighed down with anxieties, worries, and the cares of life. He reminded them that the God who clothes the simple wildflowers with such beauty knows how to care for those who daily look to Him for help, hope, and direction.

Every spring, Texans get a breathtaking reminder of God's care when they look out at the royal mantle of blue-violet bluebonnets clothing their state with beauty. In the same way, we need to open our eyes to the Father's care and attention to detail in every corner and crevice of our days—to the very horizon of our lives.

Lord God, open my eyes to see Your faithfulness and constant care in every area of my life. As best as I know how, I bring my anxieties and worries to You and leave them at Your feet. Fill my eyes and refresh my heart with reminders of Your love and tender care.

★ ★ ★

GOD'S CARE EXTENDS TO THE SMALLEST DETAILS OF OUR LIVES.

Hoover Dam
Nevada–Arizona

A QUESTION OF POWER

"In your hands are strength and power to exalt and give strength to all."
—1 CHRONICLES 29:12

When engineers set out to wrestle the mighty Colorado River into submission, they had already known for years where they would erect a dam. It would be in Black Canyon straddling the border between Arizona and Nevada. Construction began in 1931 and was completed five years later. It took over 3 1/4 million cubic yards of concrete and twenty-one thousand men to complete. At over 726 feet high and 660 feet thick at its base, it remains one of the most awesome man-made structures and engineering marvels on earth. Behind the towering dam is the reservoir known as Lake Mead—110 miles long with 550 miles of shoreline. Through the years, the lake has become one of America's favorite recreation sites, with over ten million people visiting every year. Below the dam in the U-shaped powerhouse, seventeen massive hydroelectric generators spin day and night, drawing on the channeled might of 248 square miles of water and generating up to four billion kilowatt-hours of power every year.

Imagine yourself inside this colossal power plant, each wing twenty stories high and longer than two football fields. You're standing there with your little iPhone in your hand that's in the red zone and needs a recharge. Right beside you is an outlet tapped into the gathered might of Lake Mead and Hoover Dam. Do you think you might be worried about finding adequate power to charge up your frail little smartphone? How foolish that would be! It's a good picture of what it's like when we bring our anxieties and troubling life situations to the Lord. Even though our circumstances may seem overwhelming, when we pray to our Father we are tapping into an *unlimited* reservoir of power, wisdom, and love. We can bring any and every worry and fear to Him, no matter how difficult and complicated it may seem to us, trusting Him to empower us with the help we need in His time and in His way.

Father, forgive me for my small faith and tiny expectations. Today I humbly bring all of my life situations and difficulties to You, knowing that Your power and Your love for me are far greater than I could ever begin to imagine or dream.

★ ★ ★

DON'T LET YOUR RECHARGEABLE BATTERIES
DIE IN THE MIDDLE OF A POWERHOUSE.

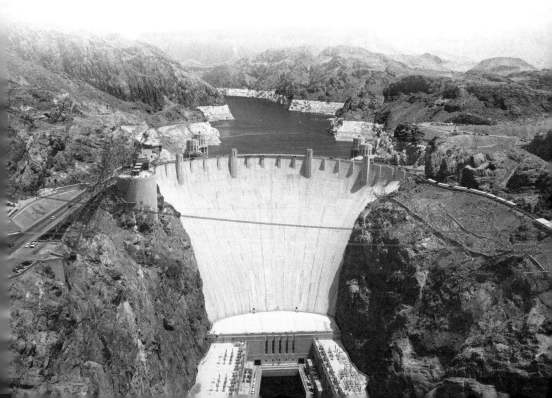

Redwood National and State Parks California

WITNESSES

*After that he was seen by more than five hundred Christian brothers at
one time, most of whom are still alive, though some have died by now.*

—1 CORINTHIANS 15:6 TLB

The California redwoods are among the oldest living things on earth. While the wind-blasted bristle-cone pine trees near the Mojave Desert may be the oldest trees of all, the redwoods create a profound *feeling* of age because of their awe-inspiring size. The Redwood National and State Parks is in Northern California, just below the Oregon border near Crescent City. This protected federal and state parkland covers 131,983 acres—although 96 percent of the original old-growth redwood forest has been decimated by logging. With ages up to two thousand years, the coastal redwoods can soar to great heights. Hyperion, at an undisclosed location in the park, is the tallest known tree in the world at 379 feet and continues to inch its way higher every year.

Two thousand years ago, a little redwood seedling pushed its way through the moist, coastal soil in what would one day be known as Northern California. At the same time, in the Roman province of Palestine, in a village called Bethlehem, a baby boy was born. Jesus lived thirty-three years before laying down His life, but the little seedling across the world continued growing, reaching a height of over 50 feet by AD 33. Among the redwoods, you can touch living trees that were already growing when Jesus was born, crucified, and raised from the dead. These were young, thriving trees when the Holy Spirit descended at Pentecost and when Paul preached to the Athenian skeptics on Mars Hill. Sometimes it seems like the words we read in our New Testament took place so long ago that they almost lose reality for us. But then you remember that there are trees alive today that were also alive when all these things took place. Was it really such a distant time? The redwoods are silent witnesses to the world-shaping events that happened two millennia ago, and they are among us today.

Lord Jesus, forgive me for allowing the truths of Your Word to become like long-ago, far-away stories in my mind. What You accomplished for me on the cross allows me to live a victorious life this very day.

REDWOODS ALIVE TODAY SHARED THE SAME SUNLIGHT AND THE SAME SKY AS JESUS OF NAZARETH.

Put-in-Bay, Ohio

PLACE OF SHELTER

I would hurry to my place of shelter,
far from the tempest and storm.

—PSALM 55:8

*P*ut-in-Bay is a small village located on South Bass Island, three miles from the shoreline of Lake Erie near Sandusky, Ohio. In the late 1700s, when schooners encountered some of the lake's infamous storms, they would "put in" to this bay on the island, finding shelter from the wind and breakers and a safe place to wait out the dangerous weather. Today, the community of Put-in-Bay is a highly popular summer resort and vacation destination, with beaches for swimming and sunbathing. Ferry and airline services connect South Bass Island with other nearby islands and Sandusky. Visitors take advantage of the walks and pathways along the downtown harbor, savoring the sunsets and watching the boats, jet skis, and ferries that come and go all summer long. In the village itself, there are shops, boutiques, restaurants, live entertainment, and even an antique carousel that's been making the rounds since 1917.

In the Bible, David spent much of his young life seeking shelter from the murderous jealousy of Israel's King Saul. As a fugitive on the run, he fled from mountain to canyon, from cave to ravine, from desert to forest. But when the strain and loneliness and fear became too much for him, he simply ran into the arms of God. In Psalm 91:1–2 he wrote, "Whoever dwells in the shelter of the Most High will rest in the shadow of the Almighty. I will say of the LORD, 'He is my refuge and my fortress.'" The Lord became a movable shelter for David. Wherever he was, David knew how to find asylum within God Himself.

We can do the same. No matter what our situation—whether we are lost in the dark, in a hospital emergency room, in a prison cell, or even in hospice—we can find shelter and safe harbor in our heavenly Father. He is our "Put-in-Bay," wherever we may sail for the rest of our days.

Father, it's so encouraging to know that my Refuge, my Hiding Place, is always with me. No matter what happens in life, I can turn to You in a heartbeat to claim Your protection, Your counsel, and Your unfailing love.

★ ★ ★

WE CAN'T ESCAPE THE STORMS, BUT WE CAN RIDE THEM OUT IN A SAFE PLACE.

Recreation Path Stowe, Vermont

THE BEST PATH

You make known to me the path of life;
you will fill me with joy in your presence,
with eternal pleasures at your right hand.

—PSALM 16:11

Stowe, Vermont, was already an idyllic New England village before the town completed its internationally acclaimed Recreation Path in 1989. The Recreation Path just made it even better. Located in the upper middle of the state, Stowe is known for skiing, arts and crafts shows, mountain biking, golf—and especially for the vivid autumn colors that wash across surrounding hills and mountains. No matter what the season, Stowe has postcard good looks complete with a picturesque white-steepled church, a covered bridge, and a winding river.

The Stowe Recreation Path is an award-winning 5.3-mile paved greenway suitable for walking, jogging, biking, rollerblading—or cross-country skiing in the winter. The path meanders through woods and pastures, past farms, barns, and shops, crossing the West Branch River on graceful bridges. In the summer, swimming holes, picnic tables, and quiet vistas along the way invite the traveler to make it a leisurely journey.

Following Jesus Christ through life is the very best course we could ever take. Solomon wrote, "The path of the righteous is like the morning sun, shining ever brighter till the full light of day" (Proverbs 4:18). Walking with God and obeying the inner direction of the Holy Spirit is the path of *life,* directing us safely through this world and leading on to the next. But that doesn't make the journey easy. In fact, our path may lead us into dangerous, slippery places, make steep climbs and sharp turns, and sometimes become so faint we can barely make it out. Our trail through the years may involve suffering, misunderstanding, pain, perplexity, and loss. But it is still the very best path. It's best because of where it leads—to everlasting life with Him in heaven. It's best because of the friendships with brothers and sisters in Christ we meet along the way. And it's best because of the One who walks with us, stride for stride. David said, "Even though I walk through the darkest valley, I will fear no evil, for you are with me" (Psalm 23:4).

Father, keep me from wandering off the path of life today. I'm so grateful You go ahead of me and walk with me.

OUR PATH MIGHT SEEM LONG, BUT IT'S REALLY
ONLY A FEW STEPS BEFORE ETERNITY.

Harpers Ferry, West Virginia

AT THE CONFLUENCE

From one man he made all the nations, that they should inhabit the whole earth; and he marked out their appointed times in history and the boundaries of their lands.

—ACTS 17:26

Harpers Ferry is a picturesque, historic community at the confluence of the Potomac and Shenandoah Rivers and the meeting place of three state boundaries: West Virginia, Virginia, and Maryland. From the very beginning, the town's location has been strategic.

It was founded in 1734 by a Quaker named Robert Harper, who in years to come set up a ferry business, carrying travelers across the Potomac River. Both Thomas Jefferson and George Washington visited the community. Jefferson wrote: "The passage of the Patowmac through the Blue Ridge is perhaps one of the most stupendous scenes in Nature . . . worth a voyage across the Atlantic." The town became a launching point for settlers headed for the Shenandoah Valley and points west, and after that, an important rail center. During the Civil War, Union and Confederate troops fought bitterly over the location, leaving destruction in their wake. Between 1864 and 1865, the town changed hands eight times.

Today the town is home to the Harpers Ferry National Historic Park, where visitors can tour historic sites and exhibits and take advantage of outdoor recreational opportunities.

By any measure, Harpers Ferry is a strategic place. *But so is where God has placed you.* You too are in a vitally important location, whether it seems that way to you or not. God had good reasons for placing you right where you are in this season of life, and He has a plan to use you. You may live in a place with critical spiritual importance in the ongoing battle between darkness and light, and God may be calling on you to pray, shine your light, and fearlessly identify with Jesus. The point is, until God clearly moves you somewhere else, this is precisely where He wants you. And there is something—right here, right now—that He wants you to do.

> *Father, I'm thankful You have a strong purpose for my life—at this time, in this place. If I have been sleepwalking and missing Your plan, please open my eyes to what You have for me.*

SINCE AN ALL-WISE GOD HAS YOU WHERE YOU ARE, IT'S THE MOST IMPORTANT PLACE YOU COULD EVER BE.

Maroon Bells Colorado

REFLECTIONS

We Christians . . . can be mirrors that brightly reflect the glory of the Lord. And as the Spirit of the Lord works within us, we become more and more like him.

—2 CORINTHIANS 3:18 TLB

The Maroon Bells are two fourteen-thousand-foot-plus peaks in the Elk Mountains, about twelve miles southwest of Aspen, Colorado. Surrounded by national forest lands, the twin peaks are said to be the most photographed mountains in all of North America. While most mountains in the Rockies consist of granite and limestone, the Bells are composed of hardened mudstone, giving the mountains a distinctive reddish tint. The view from Maroon Lake is especially stunning. Encompassed by acres of wildflowers in the summer, colorful foliage in the fall, or pristine snowfields in the winter, the lake doubles the beauty by giving back a crystal-clear reflection of the surrounding glories. The glacial valley below the peaks has limited accessibility by car, but visitors can reach this greatly loved scenic area via bus tours throughout the day during the summer season.

A murky, weed-choked pond won't give back a reflection of even the mightiest mountains that tower nearby. But a clean, calm lake surface will shine out with the image of the majesty that surrounds it. As Christians, we have little beauty or glory within ourselves. But God has given us the capacity to reflect the very personality and character qualities of Jesus Christ Himself. Romans

8:29 tells us that during our lives here on earth, we are being conformed or changed into the image of God's Son. When our hearts are still, unruffled by worries and anxieties, and we have allowed our lives to be cleansed of all known sin, we become a surface that will catch and reflect God's beauty to watching eyes all around us. People will be attracted to what they see of Jesus in our lives, much as they were attracted to Him when He walked on the earth two thousand years ago. Catching a glimpse of a compelling reflection, they will want to see the source of the Reality for themselves.

Lord Jesus, help me to reflect Your heart, Your character, and Your love to people in my life who need to see You today.

★ ★ ★

A FAITHFUL REFLECTION DRAWS THE HEART TO A BEAUTIFUL REALITY.

Hawaii Volcanoes National Park

WHEN THE MOUNTAINS CHANGE

God is our refuge and strength,
an ever-present help in trouble.
Therefore we will not fear, though the earth give way
and the mountains fall into the heart of the sea,
though its waters roar and foam
and the mountains quake with their surging.

—PSALM 46:1–3

When most people from the mainland think of Hawaii, they dream about the white sands, whispering palms, warm ocean waves, and soft trade winds. But on the big island, Hawaii has another face altogether. Hawaii Volcanoes National Park contains two active volcanoes: Kilauea and Mauna Loa. Mauna Loa lifts its bulk over 13,677 feet above the sea. Visitors to the 333,000-acre park gain spectacular views of volcanic landscapes in addition to rare glimpses of unusual flora and fauna. A few years ago, a lava flow from Kilauea pushed all the way to the ocean, creating a dramatic scene of fiery molten rock pouring into the blue Pacific, sending up huge plumes of steam.

In a normal world, mountains and oceans are stable elements of the landscape that pretty much stay where they are. But what happens when they don't? In Hawaii, you have mountains becoming liquid, slipping into the sea, turning ocean waters into a boiling cauldron. In volcanic eruptions, mountains can change shape, appear, and disappear. Whole landscapes can be transformed, with roads covered by lava and rivers diverted into new courses. That happens in our personal lives as well. Someone close to us dies, a marriage fractures, we move to a strange new city, we're let go from a job we've held for years, or some injury or illness forces us into a different way of living. Just that quickly, the comfortable, recognizable landscape changes. We feel disoriented, confused, or afraid. Today's scripture tells us that in such times, God is "a very present help." We can find a secure refuge and a steady source of strength even when our familiar world turns upside down.

Father, I know there will be eruptions in my life too—times when my landscape will shake and change. In those moments, help me to remember that You are a "very present help," and I don't have to be afraid.

★ ★ ★

MOUNTAINS MAY MOVE, BUT GOD DOESN'T. HE IS "AT THE STILL POINT OF THE TURNING WORLD."*

---

* From T. S. Elliot's "Four Quartets"

Gateway Arch
St. Louis, Missouri

THE JOURNEY BEGINS

*"The LORD, before whom I have walked faithfully, will send
his angel with you and make your journey a success."*

—GENESIS 24:40

Sites like Mount Rushmore or the Lincoln Memorial cause us to reflect—to look back—on our history and the wisdom and skill of leaders who led the nation in times of crisis. But the Gateway Arch in St. Louis, Missouri, implies forward movement. The Arch speaks of a new day and new beginnings. At 630 feet, the gleaming stainless steel monument is the tallest in the nation. The Arch was completed in 1965, and commemorates Thomas Jefferson's and St. Louis's role in the westward expansion of the United States. Visitors to the arch can ride to the top of the structure in an enclosed tram; the viewing area at the apex offers thirty miles of unparalleled views of the city and the Mississippi River.

In J. R. R. Tolkien's *The Fellowship of the Ring*, Bilbo Baggins warns his nephew, "It's a dangerous business, Frodo, going out of your door. . . . You step into the road, and if you don't keep your feet, there's no knowing where you might be swept off to." Bilbo was right. Life is never static. It keeps moving along as our situations and circumstances change by the day—or by the hour. In a very real sense, every morning of our lives is like beginning a new journey, with no two days ever alike. In Scripture, as the Israelites were about to enter the promised land, Joshua told them to carefully follow the priests carrying the ark of the covenant. "Then you will know which way to go, since you have never been this way before" (Joshua 3:4). We don't know what waits beyond our front door each day—whether trial, tragedy, unexpected blessing, or the greatest opportunity of our lives. Even so, we can begin each day's journey with prayer, placing all the details of our lives in God's hands, and leaning moment-by-moment on His Holy Spirit for guidance.

Lord God, today is a "gateway arch" to situations, problems, and opportunities I have never encountered before. Before I step under the arch, I ask for Your protection, Your favor, and Your companionship.

★ ★ ★

JESUS, OUR TOUR GUIDE, HAS ALREADY BEEN
EVERYWHERE WE WILL GO AND KNOWS THE WAY.

Savannah, Georgia

REMEMBER . . . THEN MOVE FORWARD

If My people who are called by My name will humble themselves, and
pray and seek My face, and turn from their wicked ways, then I will
hear from heaven, and will forgive their sin and heal their land.

—2 CHRONICLES 7:14 NKJV

Once you've visited, it's easy to understand why Savannah, Georgia, has been called one of the ten most beautiful cities in America. In the spring, azaleas grace the parks, gardens, and oak-lined roadways with purple, pink, and red blooms—not to mention the dogwoods lining cobbled streets and wisteria draping grand old mansions in the city's historic district. Along the Savannah River, where classic paddlewheel riverboats cruise by, there is room to stroll the walkways, looking into a variety of shops, eateries, and hotels.

Savannah is the oldest city in Georgia, dating back to 1733 when it became a British provincial capital. By the time America's Revolutionary War erupted, the city had become an important commercial port for the thirteen colonies.

However, Savannah has had its darker days, when the Southern slave trade used the city as a major port. Today's Savannah remembers its history—the good and the bad—but has set out to become one of the most creative and vigorous economic and cultural centers in the Southeast.

The Bible encourages us to remember certain things, but not to live in the past. When we think of our own past, we remember how lost we were without God and how we lived in dark places, doing and saying things we're now ashamed of. But then we remember what God has done for us in Christ, freeing us from our sin, our addictions, and our selfish ways. We remember His goodness and kindness toward us, His love, His counsel, His companionship, His provision. And then, remembering those things, we turn our focus forward, making the most of each new day and seeking to follow the Lord as closely as we can. We don't deny our past; we simply don't choose to live there.

Father, I'm reminded of how hopeless and empty my days seemed before Jesus came into my life. Thank You for not only forgiving my sins, but for also putting them out of Your memory. Thank You that I can live this day to the fullest, knowing that You are my confidence.

★ ★ ★

WE MAY GLANCE IN THE REARVIEW MIRROR, BUT OUR
STEADY FOCUS REMAINS ON THE ROAD AHEAD.

Thousand Springs State Park
Idaho

PURIFIED WATER

But he knows the way that I take;
when he has tested me, I will come forth as gold.

—JOB 23:10

The water bursting from the wall of the Snake River Canyon at a rate of 250 cubic feet per second is icy cold and incredibly pure. It has also traveled a very long way—both in distance and time. Niagara Springs is part of the world-famous Thousand Springs State Park complex along the Snake River in southern Idaho. Water from northern mountains literally disappears into the desert, absorbed by the porous volcanic soil. The underground river keeps moving, however, to the south. When the stream finally gushes out of the canyon wall above the Snake River, it has traveled over a hundred miles—*and for nearly two hundred years*. Talk about filtered water! This must be one of the sweetest, freshest drinks in America.

God's purposes and methods in our lives can be as difficult to follow as that underground river winding beneath the Idaho desert. It's hard to understand why God allows us to go through disappointments, heartbreaks, and painful trials. But over and over again, the Bible assures us that God is working behind the scenes to strengthen our faith, purify us from harmful sins, and teach us to depend more and more every day on His strength, wisdom, and love.

What keeps our hearts encouraged is to remember that "He knows the way I take," and that He who began a good work in our lives won't stop walking with us and working in us until that plan and purpose is complete (Philippians 4:6). It may not make much sense to us at times, but it will all be crystal clear someday—on this side of heaven or in His presence.

Father, I thank You that every bend and turn in my life has a place in Your good plan for me. Though Your purposes often seem invisible to me, I choose to trust You and believe that You are working out everything for my good.

WE DON'T HAVE TO BE OUR OWN TOUR GUIDE THROUGH LIFE—JESUS WANTS THAT JOB HIMSELF.

Pike Place Market
Seattle, Washington

JOYOUS VARIETY

He was given authority, glory and sovereign power; all nations
and peoples of every language worshiped him.

—DANIEL 7:14

One of the most recognizable, beloved attractions of Seattle, also known as the Emerald City, is a large public market overlooking Elliott Bay on the waterfront. Pike Place Market opened as a farmers' market in the summer of 1907 and has grown into a multilevel assortment of shops, booths, and stands selling an amazing diversity of fresh foods, specialty foods, flowers, crafts, antiques, clothing, books, and gifts. It is also home to dozens of restaurants, bakeries, bistros, and coffee shops (including the original Starbucks). The Pike Place Fish, an open-air fish market founded in 1930, is known for a tradition of its crew lobbing huge fish to one another before wrapping them up for delighted customers. Within the market—which spills out of the buildings into cobbled streets and alleys—you can meet people of many nationalities selling ethnic foods and treats from all over the world. Pike Place Market is open 362 days a year and attracts over ten million visitors every year.

If we could, at this moment, gather all the church of Jesus Christ scattered around the world and from every era of history into one place for a joint worship service, what a joyous jumble and cacophony it would be! Some would stand and lift their hands, some would dance and sway with the music, and some would bow low. You would hear every language and dialect, and see every manner of colorful outfit and garb. Someday we won't have to imagine it, because we will *experience* it when all nations will come and worship before the Lord (Revelation 15:4). The fact is that life is too short to spend time worrying about worship styles, traditions, music preferences, or what people choose to wear when Christ's people gather. We all worship the same Lord and King, who purchased us with His own blood. It's time to put away critical thoughts and words and give ourselves over to gratitude and joy.

Lord Jesus, help me to take every opportunity to learn, worship, laugh, weep, help, and share meals with this worldwide family of Yours, all those who love You and honor Your name.

★ ★ ★

THE CHURCH OF JESUS CHRIST IS A JOYOUS JUMBLE
THAT HE DAILY WEAVES TOGETHER FOR HIS GLORY.

Headwaters of the Mississippi Itasca State Park, Minnesota

HEADWATERS

"Truly I tell you, if you have faith as small as a mustard seed, you can say to this mountain, 'Move from here to there,' and it will move. Nothing will be impossible for you."

—MATTHEW 17:20

Abraham Lincoln once dubbed it "the Father of Waters." At its mouth, south and east of New Orleans, the Mississippi River discharges into the Gulf of Mexico at a rate of 844,530 cubic feet of water per second.

The mighty Mississippi has its origins in Itasca Lake in northern Minnesota. The truth is, there are more than one hundred lakes in the thirty-two thousand acres of Itasca State Park with camping, hiking, canoeing, and many other year-round recreational opportunities. But what brings millions of visitors from all over the world is the simple experience of walking twenty or thirty feet across the headwaters of the Mississippi River on stones. It's hard to get used to the idea that something so mighty that it is ranked as the tenth largest river in the world by the time it reaches the Gulf of Mexico could be so small at its source that a child can walk across it in a few steps.

The Bible speaks of faith as something that begins small but has unimaginable "downstream" effects. In Hebrews 11, the writer tells of those who "through faith conquered kingdoms, . . . shut the mouths of lions, quenched the fury of the flames, . . . and who became powerful in battle and routed foreign armies" (vv. 33–34).

It all begins with a simple decision in the heart to believe God, and act on that belief. What flows from *that* simply can't begin to be measured. Every church that's ever been founded, every ministry that's ever been launched, every powerful move of God's Spirit that's ever swept through a neighborhood, a city, or a nation began with someone believing God and moving ahead in faith. But the river gets even wider than that. The repercussions of our obedience and faith roll down through the years, beyond our lifetimes, and out of time altogether. Our tiny steps of faith may not seem like much now, but in His time, God can grow them into a river that touches eternity.

Father, I don't care about doing a great work. I just want to obey You and take the next step in faith. What flows from that is in Your hands.

A YES IN FAITH BEGINS EVERYTHING. WHERE IT ENDS CAN'T BE CALCULATED.

The Cliff Walk
Newport, Rhode Island

THE EDGE

So I say, walk by the Spirit, and you will not gratify the desires of the flesh.

—GALATIANS 5:16

One side of the path offers sheer cliffs and dramatic views of Atlantic Ocean breakers. The other side features wide stretches of green turf and mansions so massive, so splendid, that they seem to rise up out of a dream. The 3.5-mile Cliff Walk along the eastern coastline of Newport, Rhode Island, is unique in its designation as a National Recreation Trail *and* a National Historic District. Along the way, walkers have a rear view of some of Newport's most famous mansions from its Gilded Age. The first two-thirds of the walk features a paved pathway and an easy stroll with turns, tunnels, and photo-friendly coastline vistas. The final third, however, is more challenging, with unpaved portions and a rougher trail along the rocky shore. Walkers are warned to be aware and alert, taking extra caution as they go.

Every step of life on this earth is on a cliff, on the edge. We may not see the hazards, but they are there. It's a beautiful walk, but it can also be difficult and dangerous. Every one of us, no matter how faithfully we have followed Christ through the years, has the potential to give way to temptations and fall away into a life that dishonors God, ourselves, and our families. The moment we imagine ourselves to be immune to harm is the most dangerous moment of all. In the New Testament, Demas had been a loyal disciple of Christ and a valued member of Paul's mission team. He had been with Paul in Rome, sharing his difficulties and dangers (Colossians 4:14; Philemon 24). But at the very end, just when Paul needed him most, Demas bailed on the mission and went off chasing the bright, alluring lights of Thessalonica (2 Timothy 4:9–10). It could happen to any of us. If we lose focus, become distracted, or forget our priorities, the beautiful cliff walk could become a potential tragedy.

Father, please remind me where I am—so near the edge of losing all that means most to me. Help me to walk in peace and safety today by Your Spirit.

★ ★ ★

THE VIEW FROM THE CLIFF MAY BE STUNNING, BUT IT'S STILL A CLIFF.

The Biltmore Estate
Asheville, North Carolina

RARE AND BEAUTIFUL TREASURES

By wisdom a house is built,
through understanding it is established;
through knowledge its rooms are filled
with rare and beautiful treasures.

—PROVERBS 24:3-4

On Christmas Eve in 1895, George and Edith Vanderbilt opened the doors of their newly built "country retreat" to family and friends in what must have been a most memorable Christmas party. And for guests exploring the house that night, there was plenty of elbow room. To this day the magnificently furnished 250-room residence contains over four acres of floor space, including 35 bedrooms, 43 bathrooms, and 65 fireplaces. Built in the style of a French Renaissance chateau, the opulent home with its surrounding gardens is open to the public and has become a top North Carolina tourist attraction. The mansion and eight thousand-acre estate took six years to build and perfect and now, more than 120 years later, has lost little of its storied grandeur. At 178,926 square feet, Biltmore is the largest privately owned house in the United States. In self-guided tours, visitors will see displays of vintage clothing, exquisite furniture, and priceless works of art, including stunning floor-to-ceiling sixteenth-century tapestries and a ten thousand-volume library. The seventy-five-acre grounds include formal gardens, a winery, and—for those who want to linger on the estate—a cottage and 240-room hotel.

When the book of Proverbs says "by wisdom a house is built," it isn't speaking of a beautiful home, it is speaking of a beautiful life. Whether long or brief in earthly years, a life built on a foundation of belief in God and faith in Jesus Christ will stand strong through any storm, and its impact will endure (Matthew 7:24). The Proverbs 24 passage says of the wisdom-established house that "through knowledge its rooms are filled with rare and beautiful treasures." A life firmly established in Christ and following the principles of His Word will be filled with countless blessings, the evidence of His grace, and the working of His hand within the smallest details. These treasures are beyond any price and will last for eternity.

Father, I know that I am building and furnishing this life You have given me—day by day and hour by hour. Any genuine and lasting treasures in my house come from Your hands and because of Your grace.

WISDOM FOR LIFE MINED FROM THE COUNSEL OF GOD YIELDS WEALTH BEYOND PRICE.

The Durango & Silverton Narrow Gauge Railroad Colorado

THE NARROW WAY

The gateway to life is very narrow and the road is difficult, and only a few ever find it.

—MATTHEW 7:14 NLT

The Durango & Silverton Railroad is a historic narrow-gauge railway operating between the cities of Durango and Silverton in southwest Colorado. Originally built to carry supplies and people to and from the gold and silver mines in the San Juan Mountains—and to bring back the precious ore—the railroad has been designated a National Historic Landmark. The steam train, in continuous operation since 1882, now carries tourists and history enthusiasts on a scenic half-day excursion along the Animas River through Colorado wilderness inaccessible by any road.

The Durango-Silverton line winds through the canyons on a narrow-gauge, three-foot-wide track. The dictionary defines *narrow* as "of little breadth or width . . . not wide as usual or expected." When Jesus spoke of the way of salvation and the entrance to eternal life, He also described that gateway as narrow. He said, "I am the way and the truth and the life. No one comes to the Father except through me. . . . I am the gate; whoever enters through me will be saved" (John 14:6; 10:9). The gate into heaven is the width of one Person, Jesus Christ, *and no wider.* You enter into life through Him and through His sacrifice on the cross, or you don't enter at all. But when Jesus says that the way is narrow, it doesn't mean He wants His followers to be narrow. We think of "narrow-minded people" as judgmental or critical, set in their own opinions, and having little sympathy or care for others. As sons and daughters of God, however, we are called to be broad in the way we care for people, accept people, help people, and reach out to people. The way to heaven may be narrow, but those of us who point the way ought to be warm, wide-open, and welcoming.

Father, open my eyes and my heart to all kinds of people who need You. Help me not to judge and reject people that You love and want to reach.

WHILE THE MESSAGE OF SALVATION MAY BE NARROW, ITS MESSENGERS NEED WIDE-OPEN HEARTS.

Mackinac Island, Michigan

TIMES OF REFRESHING

"I will refresh the weary and satisfy the faint."

—JEREMIAH 31:25

A group of determined people made a collective decision about a place that they loved, and it remains a good decision over a century later. As early as 1898, the residents and civic leaders of Mackinac Island decided that no motorized vehicles would be allowed on their beautiful Lake Huron retreat. If people needed to get around, they could do it on foot, by bicycle, or in a horse-drawn carriage or sleigh. And those pleasant restrictions have remained in place to this day.

Almost four square miles in land area, the island is situated at the eastern end of the Straits of Mackinac, between Michigan's Upper and Lower Peninsulas. The entire island has been listed as a National Historic Landmark—a fact so easy to see in the lovingly preserved and restored homes and businesses. For year-round visitors from busier, noisier, more hectic places, Mackinac is an island of refreshment and peace.

The apostle Peter had refreshment in mind when he offered strong counsel to a group of edgy, burdened-down, uptight people. He said, "Now change your mind and attitude to God and turn to him so he can cleanse away your sins and send you wonderful times of refreshment from the presence of the Lord" (Acts 3:19 TLB). In other words, life can be different for you—and so very much better.

The change begins with your attitude toward God and those sins in your life that have separated you from Him.

"Times of refreshing from the Lord" have little to do with your circumstances, finances, health, job, or surroundings. You could be in a hospital, in rehab, in hospice, or even in jail and still experience that inner river of relief and delight that comes from a fresh or restored relationship with the living God. Seek that refreshment today. Right in the midst of your pressures, turn to Him, confessing your sins and wrong attitudes. His peace will find you wherever you are—on a lovely resort island or up to your knees in mud.

Father, I do seek "times of refreshing" from Your nearness and companionship today. Reveal to me anything in my life that might keep me from experiencing that fullness.

GOD CAN BRING A SENSE OF REFRESHMENT AND
RELIEF INTO THE VERY MIDST OF OUR TROUBLE.

High Line Park
New York City

SOMETHING NEW FROM SOMETHING OLD

"For I know the plans I have for you," declares the LORD, *"plans to prosper you and not to harm you, plans to give you hope and a future."*

—JEREMIAH 29:11

*B*ack in the 1960s, somewhere in the Midwest, someone had a truly breakthrough idea: turn a local abandoned railroad track into a public walking trail. That idea has caught on all across the nation, giving Americans what they'd never really had before . . . a network of trails for strolling, hiking, and biking.

Maybe going one step further is a dramatic example of "rails to trails" in New York City, where a group of dedicated volunteers, partnering with a railroad company, the city, and private investors, has turned a 1.45' mile section of a disused and derelict New York Central Railroad spur—the West Side Line—into a delightful park up above the city streets in Manhattan. The elevated trail includes carefully selected grass, trees, shrubs, flowers, and benches and artwork, cafes and coffee shops. It features leisurely, one-of-a-kind vistas of the Hudson River and the New York City skyline, complete with security officers who keep everything peaceful and safe.

What's most encouraging is that city and community planners have taken something neglected and abandoned and *repurposed* it into a place of beauty and tranquility above the hustle and congestion of America's busiest city.

It's a picture of what God does for you and me. He is the One who can take our abandoned plans, broken dreams, and disappointed desires and make something useful and beautiful from our lives. This is the God who gives "a crown of beauty instead of ashes, the oil of joy instead of mourning, and a garment of praise instead of a spirit of despair" (Isaiah 61:3). Maybe life hasn't turned out the way we had hoped or expected, but whoever we are and whatever our circumstances, God can bring unexpected good out of plans we'd given up as lost. In New York, it didn't happen until the railroad company let go of the old property. In our lives, it doesn't happen until we place everything—all we are and have—into the hands of our Creator and Savior.

Father, help me to release all of my hopes, plans, and expectations—as well as my false starts, stumbles, and disappointments—into Your good hands and Your safekeeping. I trust You to bring usefulness, fresh purpose, and a renewed zest for life to this day, this precious, irreplaceable day that You have given me.

★ ★ ★

OUR DREAMS ARE NEVER SAFER THAN WHEN LEFT IN HIS HANDS.

Charleston, South Carolina

POSITIONED FOR BLESSING

Therefore the LORD longs to be gracious to you,
And therefore He waits on high to have compassion on you. . . .
How blessed are all those who long for Him.

—ISAIAH 30:18 NASB

For an American city, Charleston's roots go *way* back. The oldest and second-largest city in South Carolina, the community was founded in 1670 and named Charles Town in honor of the English king, Charles II. Located halfway down the state's Atlantic coastline on Charleston Harbor, the city has a population of nearly 130,000 and is one of the state's fastest-growing municipalities and a major tourist destination. Even so, it hasn't forgotten its history or refined southern manners. "Charleston," says one writer, "is not only steeped in history, but it also is oozing with charm."*

Many of the city's distinctive, historic homes were built on long, narrow lots with the sides of the homes, rather than the fronts, facing the streets. Porches run the length of the houses. Why were these homes positioned with sides to the streets? The most practical reason was to keep the houses cool on hot, humid days before the advent of air-conditioning or electric fans. When the welcome prevailing southerly winds would blow through the city from the Atlantic, they would sweep the houses from end to end. The houses, then, are perfectly positioned to receive the blessing of cooling sea breezes.

---

* http://lancasteronline.com/lifestyle/charleston-s-charms/article_1b322c7a-9100-52d5-b6b2-6c62f8ae74fd.html

Just as those historic Charleston homes counted on prevailing breezes from the sea, we as believers depend on the flow of God's goodness and blessings into our daily lives. David wrote, "How abundant are the good things that you have stored up for those who fear you" (Psalm 31:19). If our lives feel empty, desolate, or out of the flow of His companionship, it isn't because God isn't blessing us; it's because we've put ourselves out of position to fully receive all that He has waiting for us. If we are bitter and unforgiving toward others, we position ourselves away from receiving His forgiveness (Matthew 6:15). If we hold on to anxieties and cares instead of giving them to God, we won't receive the peace that surpasses all understanding (Philippians 4:6–7). If we stubbornly refuse to change our minds about something He convicts us to change, we won't experience the "times of refreshing" He promises (Acts 3:19).

Just as residents in Charleston opened their unconventional windows to receive the breezes from the sea, we need to prepare ourselves to open our hearts to experience the love God is more than willing to send our way.

Lord, today I want to put myself in position to receive all You intend for me in Your love.

**THE REFRESHING WIND NEEDS THE
COOPERATION OF OPEN WINDOWS.**

Monument Valley, Utah

UNTOUCHED BY THE YEARS

For I am not ashamed of the gospel, because it is the power of God that brings salvation to everyone who believes.

—ROMANS 1:16

If you were to travel back in time three hundred years to Monument Valley in the southeast portion of (what is now) the state of Utah, it would look pretty much the same as it does today. You would see a huge blue-sky horizon, great empty stretches of desert, deep red-rock canyons, and towering buttes, mesas, and sandstone formations thrusting up to a thousand feet into the air. If the magnificent panorama you witness in this thirty thousand-acre Navajo Tribal Park near the border of Arizona and Utah looks a little familiar to you, there's a good reason for it. You've probably seen that iconic landscape in countless postcards and calendars, as well as in numerous classic Western movies. Although much of the magnificent scenery can be viewed from main roads, additional sightseeing tours are available—whether on foot, by air, in a jeep, or on horseback.

If Monument Valley hasn't changed much through the centuries, the gospel of Jesus Christ hasn't changed at all. Its power was exactly the same a thousand years ago, whether communicated in North Africa, Ireland, Rome, or Constantinople. Whoever heard the gospel of Jesus Christ and understood and believed it experienced instantaneous salvation. When people heard and received the message five hundred years ago, the outcome was the same. Lives were miraculously transformed. Eternal destinies were changed. And if someone in your city, down your own street, hears and accepts the good news this afternoon, the same mighty, life-giving power will surge through his or her life as well. As Paul wrote, the gospel is "the power of God that brings salvation." So much in our world erodes or alters with the passing years, but not the gospel. Nothing about the way the world has changed in the last two thousand years has done anything to blunt, fade, detract from, or dilute the power of that message.

Father, I thank You that as long as life remains for anyone, anywhere on earth, there is a potential for immediate, permanent, eternal transformation in the gospel of Jesus Christ.

★ ★ ★

THE MOST IMPORTANT TRUTH EVER ANNOUNCED HAS 100 PERCENT OF ITS ORIGINAL IMPACT.

The Pacific Coast Highway California

SURPRISES AROUND EVERY BEND

*"I came so they can have real and eternal life, more
and better life than they ever dreamed of."*

—JOHN 10:10 MSG

The section of California State Route 1 that runs along the Pacific Coast from Monterey in the north to Santa Barbara in the south has been called one of the greatest drives in the world—and "America's most popular road trip." It's easy to see why. Hugging the rugged, dramatic California coastline, the two-lane Pacific Coast Highway (or PCH) offers attraction on top of attraction. The 458-mile trip feels a little like driving through an endless succession of photographic postcards with picturesque towns, white sandy beaches, thundering blue Pacific waves, and wind-sculpted cypress trees.

After Monterey and Carmel-by-the-Sea, the road winds through Point Lobos, Big Sur, Garrapata State Park, Ragged Point, San Simeon, Morro Bay, San Luis Obispo, and on it goes. The views are stunning, but if you're behind the wheel, you can't take your eyes off the road for very long. PCH was deliberately built to cling to the farthest western edge of the American continent, following the contours of the coastline. And that means an abundance of bends, turns, dips, quick ascents, and narrow bridges.

Some people expect their walk with God to be a sedate, sleepy stroll along a garden path. But that's not real life—and that's not what the Bible promises. When we surrender the keys of our lives to Jesus Christ, when we determine to live by faith, trusting Him to lead us and meet our needs, we shouldn't anticipate a straight road and a peaceful journey. God's ways aren't our ways, and we ought to expect the unexpected. Along the way, the Lord asks us to stay alert and be ready for sudden accelerations, quick stops, sharp bends in the highway. And when we can tear our eyes off the yellow line for a moment or two, He invites us to soak in the wonder of His creation and the sheer comfort of His constant companionship.

Father, I won't mind the quick turns, steep cliffs, and narrow bridges if I can just remember that You are with me for every mile of this journey. Help me to stay alert and undistracted—especially when we're driving in the dark.

LIFE IN CHRIST ISN'T AN EASY ROAD TRIP—
BUT THE DESTINATION IS GLORIOUS, AND SO IS
HIS COMPANIONSHIP ALONG THE WAY.

The Sandhills Nebraska

A PRAIRIE WHISPER

*The LORD passed by . . . but the LORD was not in the wind; and after the wind an
earthquake, but the LORD was not in the earthquake; and after the earthquake
a fire, but the LORD was not in the fire; and after the fire a still small voice.*

—1 KINGS 19:11–12 NKJV

The Nebraska Sandhills is a unique grassland spanning 19,600 miles of
rolling sand dunes in north-central Nebraska, covering over a quarter of
the state. Because the soil is too sandy for crops, most of this vast prairie has
never been plowed and remains blanketed with native grasses and wildflowers.
Designated a National Historic Landmark, the area is home to a wide variety of animals, including coyotes, deer, pronghorn antelope, jackrabbits, and
prairie dogs. It is also a region of abundant water. Lying just beneath the wind-sculpted hills is the Ogallala Aquifer—the largest in America—and the source of
spring-fed rivers, creeks, lakes, ponds, and wetlands. Recreational opportunities include hiking, biking, hunting, fishing, ATV trail rides, and an excellent
variety of golf courses.

Father Val Peters, director of Boys Town in Omaha, once wrote: "Anyone
can sit back at the seashore and be inspired, because it shouts at you. But the
prairie only whispers. You must listen closely and not miss the message."* And

* *http://www.discoveramerica.com/usa/experiences/n/nebraska/the-sandhills-of-nebraska.aspx*

so it is sometimes with the voice of the Holy Spirit in the life of a Christian. For most believers, the voice of the Spirit is understated and in the background. In other words, you must *listen* for His voice. It may mean tuning out the external sounds and chatter so common in today's world. When God wanted to speak to Abraham about his future, He took him for a walk out under the stars (Genesis 15:5). When David felt overwhelmed by the uproar of his world, the Lord told him to "be still, and know that I am God" (Psalm 46:10). More than ever, we need times when we deliberately seek a quiet place to listen for the voice of One who loves us more than anyone.

Thank You, Father, for the wise, steady, loving voice of Your Spirit. Quiet my heart and open my ears to hear everything You have to say to me today.

STEPPING BACK FROM THE MANY VOICES IN LIFE MAKES ROOM FOR THE ONE BEST VOICE.

Lewes, Delaware

WHAT IT MEANS TO BE FIRST

"Anyone who wants to be first must be the very last, and the servant of all."

—MARK 9:35

Lewes, Delaware, is a small coastal community near the mouth of Delaware Bay on the Atlantic coast. The town boasts of attractions many other beach towns along the Eastern Seaboard might also claim: sandy beaches, historic lighthouses, boating, bike paths, a marina, a state park, succulent seafood, and some excellent museums. Lewes, however, lays claim to something more. The town proudly owns the title of "the first town in the first state." In fact, Lewes was the earliest settlement in the state, and Delaware was the first state to ratify the United States Constitution. Back as far as 1631, Lewes was the site for an early Dutch settlement. By 1680, the settlement was in English hands and remained so until its independence in 1776. Today visitors from across America savor the small-town atmosphere, the beautiful shoreline, the scenic trails, and the fun of visiting "America's first town."

There is something about being first. Our first president, George Washington, was eulogized as "first in war, first in peace, and first in the hearts of his countrymen." In 1926, American Gertrude Ederle was the first woman to swim the English Channel, and in 1969 Neil Armstrong was the first human being to set foot on the moon. The first person to accomplish something extraordinary will often be remembered and honored by history. Jesus, however, told us that God takes special note of some who are deliberately last. "Many who are first will be last," Jesus said, "and many who are last will be first" (Matthew 19:30). Those in the latter group might have claimed the first spot in line or the first share of the applause and rewards but chose not to, allowing others to move ahead of them. They surrender their time, fame, and privileges, letting go of safety, comfort, and status for Christ's sake, to help or protect someone else. Some even lay down their lives in a world where it may or may not be noticed. But the Lord notices, and that is enough.

Jesus, You left the first and best place to put Yourself in the last and worst place, the cross, and You did it for me.

TAKING LAST PLACE FOR THE LOVE OF JESUS IS A SWEET SPOT, AND HE WILL NEVER FORGET IT.

Everglades National Park Florida

A SEARCH FOR SOLID GROUND

I waited patiently for the LORD;
he turned to me and heard my cry.
He lifted me out of the slimy pit,
out of the mud and mire;
he set my feet on a rock
and gave me a firm place to stand.

—PSALM 40:1–2

Part of what makes traveling in the United States so endlessly interesting is the mind-boggling diversity of landscapes. In the Everglades National Park of south Florida, the visitor will encounter an environment that is unique in a thousand ways. The park stretches across 1.5 million acres, providing a habitat for many threatened and endangered birds, mammals, reptiles, and insects. The park is a valuable tropical/subtropical wetland—essentially the lower half of a vast watershed that eventually drains into Florida Bay.

Those exploring the fringes of this expansive protected area can hike, canoe, camp, and sign up for tram and boat tours. Numerous elevated wooden walkways, wheelchair-accessible, add yet another opportunity to venture into this intriguing world.

If you were ever lost somewhere deep in the Everglades with night coming on, one thing you might highly value is some firm ground beneath your feet. A place to stand. A place to rest. For many people in our world looking for something true and sturdy and dependable, it's hard to find a reliable place to stand. Contemporary culture teaches that there are no absolute truths, no ultimate values, no changeless rights and wrongs, and no God in heaven who will hold people accountable for their actions. For people trying to find their way through life, the footing is soft, squishy, and sometimes frightening.

Thankfully, God has given us His Word, the Bible. The psalmist wrote, "Your word, LORD, is eternal; it stands firm in the heavens" (Psalm 119:89). We *do* have absolute truths and promises we can stand on—through life and beyond. God's Word, God's promises, and God's character never change, and we can stand—and rest—on that fact.

Father God, thank You for pulling me out of the mud and mire (again and again) and giving me a firm place to stand. Thank You that Your Word is true, solid, and completely reliable when so much else in this world seems to shift and slide, morph and change.

★ ★ ★

THE WORD OF GOD IS A FIRM AND ELEVATED
WALKWAY THROUGH TODAY'S SWAMP.

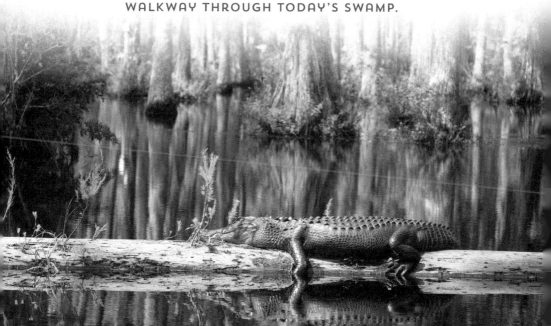

Hells Canyon National Recreation Area
Idaho and Oregon

THE DEPTHS

Out of the depths I cry to you, LORD.

—PSALM 130:1

The Wild West doesn't get any wilder than Hells Canyon—North America's deepest river gorge—knifing through the borders of western Idaho and northeastern Oregon. The terrain is so rugged and demanding that even three members of the Lewis and Clark expedition turned back from exploring it and never saw the deepest parts of the gorge. Carved by the mighty Snake River, the area covers over 652,488 acres. The canyon runs a little more than one hundred miles from Hells Gate State Park, near Lewiston, Idaho, to the Hells Canyon Dam, and in one place measures a mile and a half from the river bottom to the mountaintop above. Although the area is remote with few roads, it attracts white-water rafters, jet boaters, anglers, hikers, and campers from around the world, and boasts nine hundred miles of hiking trails, mostly on the Oregon side.

Sometimes the situations in which we find ourselves seem very deep. The river of life sweeps us into a canyon, and the walls around us soar higher and higher. Soon the cliffs are unscalable, and the sky looks like a narrow strip far above us. It could be problems with our health, with our finances, on our job, or in our closest and dearest relationships. Some people wrestle with bouts of crippling depression. Before we know it, we can be in the depths and wonder how we will ever get through it. David, the psalmist, learned something about those depths that gave him comfort. He learned that God Himself was there with him. In Psalm 139:7–8 he wrote: "Where can I go from your Spirit? Where can I flee from your presence? If I go up to the heavens, you are there; if I make my bed in the depths, you are there." And there's something else. The Snake River eventually emerges from Hells Canyon into a wider, flatter, more peaceful landscape. Yes, the canyon is deep, but the river runs through it and out the other side. God is with us in the depths, and He *will* see us through.

Father God, that's all I need to know right now. No matter how deep the canyon,
You are there with me, and You will bring me out on the other side.

BETTER TO BE IN A CANYON WITH JESUS THAN
ON A MOUNTAINTOP WITHOUT HIM.

Route 66, USA

A WELL-MARKED HIGHWAY

Whether you turn to the right or to the left, your ears will hear
a voice behind you, saying, "This is the way; walk in it."

—ISAIAH 30:21-22

US Highway 66 has worn a number of different nicknames since it was bulldozed, graveled, and eventually paved across a wide swath of the United States. It's been called Mother Road. The Main Street of America. The Will Rogers Highway. Down through the decades, however, most people who have driven, biked, walked, or hitchhiked its vast length have known it simply as "Route 66."

Although officially opened on November 11, 1926, the familiar road signs didn't appear until a year later. Several years after that, the 2,448-mile highway was completely paved all the way from Chicago to Los Angeles. Slicing across the continent and spanning eight states, the highway passed through small towns and major cities, as well as wide deserts and lonesome prairies. Owners of "Mom and Pop" stores, motels, cafes, souvenir shops, and gas stations counted on the Mother Road to bring business to their isolated communities.

In 1964, you could hear Chuck Berry on the car radio singing, "Get your kicks on Route 66." You could watch *Route 66* on TV from 1960 to 1964. The highway was finally decommissioned in 1985, already swallowed up or bypassed by America's Interstate Freeway System, with some sections being abandoned and others becoming state roads or local roads.

Several times in the Old Testament Prophets, God spoke about His wandering, scattered people finally getting back on the right highway—the well-marked road that led to a close walk with Him. It's a reminder to all of us that the way to closeness with God and the love we once had for Him isn't hard to find. No matter what detours you've taken, how far you may have wandered, or how turned around you've become in your life, you can always turn around and start back home. The road to fellowship with God is always open, and if you look for it, you will find it. In Jeremiah 29:13–14, the Lord says, "You will seek me and find me when you seek me with all your heart. I will be found by you."

Father, You know my tendency to wander away from You. One detour seems to lead to another until I've lost my way and forgotten what life is all about. Guide my feet today back to the "Father Road," and to fresh horizons and new adventures with You.

AT ANY TIME OF OUR LIVES, WE ARE ONE STEP AWAY FROM RETURNING TO INTIMACY WITH GOD.

Plymouth Rock
Plymouth, Massachusetts

REMEMBER AND RETURN

*"Go back to what you heard and believed at first; hold
to it firmly. Repent and turn to me again."*

—REVELATION 3:3 NLT

Your first reaction upon viewing Plymouth Rock on Water Street in Plymouth, Massachusetts, might be, "You mean that's *it?*" The rock itself, chiseled with the date "1620" on its face, isn't very impressive. What that rock marks, however, has significance for every American. In his iconic 1877 painting, *The Landing of the Pilgrims*, Henry A. Bacon portrayed Pilgrim men and women in a rowboat landing on a flat gray rock under a cloudy sky. Back in Plymouth harbor, you can see their ship, the *Mayflower*, riding at anchor. It was in 1620 when a group of men and women from England first set foot on the American continent. The actual rock where they stood, or what's left of it, is still on display. After being divided several times and chipped away through the years by souvenir hunters, it's hardly more than a boulder today. Even so, nearly a million people from all over the world come every year to visit "The Rock," where the United States of America began.

Returning to landmarks in our lives could be a good idea. If you find you are losing your way, it's a good plan to return to where you started. Find something familiar, get your bearings again, think about where you got off course, and then go on from there. That was essentially the Lord's message to several churches in the book of Revelation: *remember and return*. Jesus said, "Look how far you have fallen! Turn back to me and do the works you did at first." And again, "Go back to what you heard and believed at first; hold to it firmly. Repent and turn to me again" (Revelation 2:5; 3:3 NLT). Return, Jesus is saying, to your first commitments. The day when you accepted Christ as your personal Savior and your heart overflowed with new purpose, passion, and healing . . . the day you said your wedding vows and all you could think about was celebrating each day with your new spouse . . . the day you turned from an addiction or overcame a disease and you rejoiced at your second chance in life. Return and remember, then move forward again with a fresh sense of purpose.

> *Lord Jesus, I can remember "Plymouth Rock" moments in my life when I promised to love and serve You. Bring me back to those times when You meant more to me than anything else in life.*

WHEN YOU LOSE YOUR WAY, GO BACK TO WHERE
YOU LEFT THE PATH AND START AGAIN.

The Blue Ridge Parkway
North Carolina

TAKING TIME

*"In repentance and rest is your salvation,
in quietness and trust is your strength."*

—ISAIAH 30:15

*I*f you were to meet a resident from North Carolina and in casual conversation ask, "What's the best place for a drive in your state?" chances are the reply would be, "Oh, no question. It's the Blue Ridge Parkway."

They would be referring to the historic highway that weaves its way through 469 miles of incomparable American beauty, from the Shenandoah Valley in Virginia to the Smoky Mountains in North Carolina. It's known as "America's favorite drive," but don't plan on rounding those thousands of curves in a big hurry since the speed limit is forty-five miles per hour.

This isn't a journey to be rushed anyway. In fact, the route was designed from the very beginning to be savored. From Cumberland Gap to Linn Cove Viaduct, the highway features some of the most photographed vistas in America. In autumn, the vivid red, gold, and orange leaves of oak, hickory, buckeye, and ash cover the hills and mantle the mountains. In spring, rhododendrons, dogwood, buttercups, and trilliums smile a welcome around every turn of the road. When you're on the parkway, destinations are an afterthought; what counts is the journey. It's not the "getting there" that's important, it's the *being* there.

Many of us spend much of our days aiming at an end-point: finishing a project, completing a task, achieving a goal, or arriving at a destination. In the process, we miss simply tasting, savoring, and taking delight in all of God's blessings on our doorstep *today*. Where has God placed me? Who are the people around me right now? What opportunities has God set before me in this season of life? What sights, sounds, flavors, experiences, and wonders has He planned for me this very day?

In Psalm 46:10, the Lord says, "Be still, and know that I am God." In other words, slow down, literally "cease striving," and make the most of the vistas on this very curve of the highway.

Dear Lord, I'm often like Martha—preoccupied, distracted, and "worried and upset about many things."* Please help me to take my foot off the accelerator. Help me to slow down and really live today, enjoying and valuing the people, places, and circumstances immediately before me.

★ ★ ★

**LIVE THIS DAY AS IF IT WERE YOUR LAST,
SAVORING ALL THAT GOD HAS GIVEN YOU.**

---

*Luke 10:41

Flathead Lake
Montana

CLARITY

We have made this perfectly clear to you in every way.

—2 CORINTHIANS 11:6

Montana's Flathead Lake, less than ten miles from Kalispell, is the largest natural freshwater lake west of the Mississippi. The lake, with depths over 300 feet, covers 190 square miles in the northwest corner of Montana, boasting a 160-mile shoreline. Amazingly clear, it is said to be one of the cleanest lakes of its size and type anywhere in populated areas of the world. The technical explanation for the lake's clarity involves a lack of certain nutrients that promote the growth of algae. Thousands of summer visitors make the trek to Flathead Lake State Park, where they can choose from camping, picnicking, boating, hiking, fishing, or swimming—with two ultra-scenic golf courses nearby.

It would be nice if life could be as clear and transparent as Flathead Lake, enabling us to peer into the depths and make wise, far-seeing decisions. But it rarely seems to work that way. Most of the time we humans have to get along with severely limited visibility and make our choices with only a vague, somewhat cloudy view of what we should do or which way we should go. We sympathize with the apostle Paul, who said, "Now we see things imperfectly, like puzzling reflections in a mirror. . . . All that I know now is partial and incomplete" (1 Corinthians 13:12 NLT). Our point of view can be warped by our emotions, our prejudices, our hormones, our medications, our circumstances, and even by what we had for breakfast. We long for clarity and conviction, but we often have to rely on opinions and hunches. If we can't be clear in ourselves, however, we can spend time with Someone who sees with perfect clarity. Someone who has never known one split second of confusion, indecision, or perplexity. The more time we invest in Bible reading and prayer, the more we will have access to God's clear thinking. As the psalmist declared, "I have more insight than all my teachers, for I meditate on your statutes" (Psalm 119:99).

Father, please lead me by the hand today, because it's all a blur ahead of me, and I can't see where to go. Your vision and Your insights, Father, are good enough for both of us.

GOD ALLOWS US MOMENTS OF UNUSUAL CLARITY AS WE EARNESTLY SEEK HIS PERSPECTIVE.

Mount Rainier National Park Washington

SUDDEN MAJESTY

Golden splendor comes from the mountain of God.
He is clothed in dazzling splendor.
We cannot imagine the power of the Almighty.

—JOB 37:22-23 NLT

For the rookie hiker, Second Burroughs Mountain on the sunrise side of Mount Rainier offers both a difficult challenge and a reward you will never forget. Starting off from the Sunrise Visitor Center on an August morning, you will see banks of lupine, marsh marigolds, pearly everlasting, and Indian paintbrush. You may spot a lazy marmot on a flat rock soaking up the summer warmth. But suddenly the trail climbs and winds through meadows, tundra, subalpine firs, and stubborn patches of last winter's snow.

As the morning wears on, you may find yourself shedding your jacket in the heat, tripping over rocks and roots in the dusty trail, nursing blistered feet, or swatting hungry mosquitos. And then, rounding a long bend in the trail, you encounter the sight of a lifetime. Mount Rainier leaps into view, utterly dominating the horizon—14,400 feet high—and appearing beautiful beyond words. There is nothing—not so much as a twig, branch, or flower stem—between you and one of the most regal mountains in America. It's just you and that mountain in all its majesty.

So it is in our walk with God. We can trudge along through days, even years, and the way seems winding and steep. The sun bears down, obstacles trip our feet, and hope is diminished. We feel tired and discouraged and begin to wonder if the long hike is even worth the price. And then something remarkable and surprising happens. It might be in a quiet moment alone . . . swept up in worship . . . in a sudden insight from Scripture . . . or on the heels of a stunning answer to prayer. We catch a glimpse of our loving and faithful God. And He is greater than we ever knew before, more beautiful than we ever dreamed, more majestic than we could imagine. We feel His great love for us, dominating the horizon of our lives.

Father God, I find myself a little weary on the path today. Sometimes it feels more like slogging or shuffling along than running a race. I need a glimpse of You today—a fresh awareness of Your power, Your nearness, and Your love. Open my eyes of faith, Father, and give me new strength for a new day.

A GLIMPSE OF GOD OVERWHELMS US WITH HIS MAJESTY.

Indianapolis Motor Speedway Indiana

FAST AND SLOW

*My dear brothers and sisters, take note of this: Everyone should
be quick to listen, slow to speak and slow to become angry.*

—JAMES 1:19

The Indianapolis Motor Speedway (IMS) has been called the greatest race-course in the world and is home to the Indianapolis 500 and the Brickyard 400. Since it opened in 1909, the IMS has hosted some of the greatest legends in auto racing history from all over the world. No baseball or football stadium in America comes close to the seating capacity of the speedway, which is estimated at over 257,000—and 400,000 with infield seating added. That would be like seating the whole population of Cleveland, Ohio. The size of the speedway is stunning. Promoters boast that you could fit the Roman Coliseum, Vatican City, Wimbledon Campus, the Rose Bowl, Yankee Stadium, and Churchill Downs inside its 2.5-mile oval. Small wonder the Indy promoters call it "The Greatest Spectacle in Racing." In the 2014 Indianapolis 500, American Ryan Hunter-Reay averaged over 186 miles per hour. By contrast, Ray Harroun, driving his Marmon Wasp, won the race in 1911 at an average speed of 74.6 miles per hour.

When it comes to speed in our personal lives, the apostle James sets forth a simple guideline in today's Scripture: we are to be quick to listen, slow to speak, and slow to become angry. The word for *quick* in the original language means swift, prompt, ready to go. In other words, we're at the starting line, our engines are revving, and when the green flag waves, we're to open our ears and listen! When someone speaks to us, whether a spouse, child, friend, or stranger, we're ready to hear this person out, without impatience or interruption. At the same time, we are to be slow to speak—and very, very slow to lose our temper. This is like a yellow flag at the speedway, signaling a major slowdown ahead. This means being unhurried to contradict, criticize, show off our own knowledge, utter that sharp word, or to let anger overtake us.

Dear Lord, how often I have this backward! I'm slow to listen, quick to get irritable, and quick to open my mouth. As You do so often, Lord, please rearrange the priorities of my heart.

ATTENTIVE, COMPASSIONATE LISTENING IS ONE OF THE BIGGEST PARTS OF LOVE.

The Freedom Trail
Boston, Massachusetts

A PATH MARKED IN RED

"Stop at the crossroads and look around.
Ask for the old, godly way, and walk in it.
Travel its path, and you will find rest for your souls."

—JEREMIAH 6:16 NLT

The path is marked in red. Winding its way through downtown Boston, the Freedom Trail is a two-and-a-half-mile walking path linking sixteen of our nation's most renowned historic landmarks. Boston has always taken pride in its revolutionary past. But in 1954, local journalist William Schofield came up with a Revolutionary idea of his own: Since most of those significant historic sites were in close proximity, why not *link* them with a single pedestrian trail so that visitors could explore all of those landmarks in one self-guided tour? That's what the city of Boston did, and countless visitors from around the world have walked the Freedom Trail ever since.

Stops along the path include the Boston Common, the Old Statehouse, the site of the Boston Massacre, the Bunker Hill Monument, and in Boston Harbor, the historic frigate *USS Constitution*, fondly known as "Old Ironsides." All that visitors need to do is follow the narrow red path. Special markers implanted in the sidewalk denote the important stops along the way. Before the Freedom Trail, visitors armed with maps and guidebooks wandered here and there in Boston, finding a few of the sites, but probably becoming lost, confused, and missing many. The red path has made it simple.

When it comes to finding a relationship with God and a path to heaven, God made it so simple a little child could find the way. Jesus said, "I am the way and the truth and the life. No one comes to the Father except through me" (John 14:6). The Freedom Trail through life and all the way to heaven was made possible by Jesus, the One who painted the red line with His own blood given for us on the cross.

Father, thank You for the red trail, so clearly marked, that leads to heaven. I'm so thankful that You didn't leave me to wander here and there looking for the way. I would have never found it! But through the blood of Your own Son, You have shown me the way into life—and the life to come.

THE PATHWAY TO ETERNAL LIFE MAY BE NARROW,
BUT IT IS CLEARLY MARKED—IN RED.

White Mountains New Hampshire

EXPECTANT

In the morning, LORD, you hear my voice;
in the morning I lay my requests before you
and wait expectantly.

—PSALM 5:3

They're called "leaf peepers," and they've always been a fact of life in September and October in the towns, villages, roadways, and hiking trails of New Hampshire's White Mountains. They come from nearby Boston and New York City, but also from every corner of America—and beyond. Leaf peepers by the tens of thousands watch their calendars, anticipating a trip into the White Mountains to witness the autumn glory of the leaves at their peak. The state even provides a smartphone app that will tell you when the foliage in various parts of the state is at its very, very best. As the prime weeks approach, tourists will have suitcases packed and be ready to tour the little towns, wind their way along mountain roads, snap pictures of the many natural wonders, and soak in the incomparable beauty of New Hampshire in all its glory.

Leaf peepers have high expectations and are rarely disappointed. In today's scripture, David brings his requests to the Lord every morning and then eagerly watches to see how God will work things out for him. He knows he has been heard. He knows God cares for him. He knows God can accomplish anything. He knows God will work on his behalf. The fun part is waiting and watching to see *how* the Lord will do it! The word for "expectation" in Hebrew speaks of peering into the distance or watching the horizon. That's the sort of attitude, the sort of expectant faith, that pleases the Lord. It's the faith of King Jehoshaphat facing a massive army marching on an unprepared Jerusalem. In his prayer before the whole nation the king said, "We have no power to face this vast army that is attacking us. We do not know what to do, but our eyes are on you" (2 Chronicles 20:12). He didn't know how God would answer his prayer, but he just knew that somehow, some way, He would.

Father, sometimes I pray little and expect little. Open my heart today to pray much and expect even more.

★ ★ ★

I HAVE NO IDEA HOW GOD WILL WORK.
I ONLY KNOW THAT HE WILL.

Nantucket Island, Massachusetts

OUT OF THE FOG

We don't yet see things clearly. We're squinting in a fog, peering through a mist.
But it won't be long before the weather clears and the sun shines bright!

—1 CORINTHIANS 13:12 MSG

Nantucket has everything a vacationer could desire. First of all, it's an island, separated from mainland traffic and congestion by thirty miles of ocean, with access limited to airplane, boat, or ferry. In addition to pristine beaches, Nantucket offers enticing restaurants, shops and boutiques, charming inns and hotels, miles of hiking and biking trails, a wide variety of water sports, and a rich maritime history with museums and historical sites. But Nantucket also has fog. A bumper sticker you will sometimes see on the island states the obvious: FOG HAPPENS. While the fog is simply a temporary inconvenience to most people, it has also resulted in hundreds of shipwrecks off the island. These include the 1956 loss of the Italian ocean liner, *Andrea Doria*, which sank off the coast after being rammed by a Swedish freighter in the fog, with a loss of fifty-three lives.

When heavy fog descends, any travel becomes difficult. It's treacherous to drive when you can't even see a car length in front of you. Flights get delayed or canceled. Ships at sea rely heavily on instruments. If possible, the best thing to do with fog is to wait it out. Sooner or later, the curtain will part and sunlight and illumination will break through.

Sometimes, our way in life seems shrouded with fog, and decisions don't come easy. If we're forced to choose, then we have to trust God and make the best choice we can. But when the fog is heavy and the decision can be delayed, it's good to simply wait on God to make the way clear. David, who had to wait fifteen long, lonely years for the promise of his kingship, wrote, "Wait on the Lord; be of good courage, and He shall strengthen your heart; wait, I say, on the Lord!" (Psalm 27:14 NKJV). To wait on God means to focus our hope and expectation on Him, even when our choices aren't clear and circumstances aren't working out the way we had hoped.

Lord, forgive me for trying to force events or make things happen instead of waiting on You to make the way plain.

GOD'S WAY AND GOD'S WILL CAN'T BE FORCED OR HURRIED.

Crater Lake National Park Oregon

A GOD SO DEEP

May you have the power to understand . . . how wide, how long,
how high, and how deep his love is. May you experience the love
of Christ, though it is too great to understand fully.

—EPHESIANS 3:18–19 NLT

Set like a sapphire in the Cascade Mountains of Oregon, Crater Lake must surely be one of the most beautiful places on earth. At 1,943 feet, it is the deepest lake in the United States, and the seventh-deepest lake in the world. Geologists say the lake formed over seven thousand years ago, following the mighty volcanic eruption of 12,000-foot Mount Mazama. Through the centuries, the massive caldera left behind filled with rainwater and melted snow. Today, the great crater holds 4.6 trillion gallons of remarkably pure water. Those who see the lake on a clear day say that its waters define the word *blue*. Visitors can look down over encircling cliffs almost 2,000 feet high into the depths of the lake and its two islands.

The Lord once asked Job, "Have you journeyed to the springs of the sea or walked in the recesses of the deep?" (Job 38:16). Job had never done that, but God has. Down at the roots of the crater that was once Mount Mazama, almost 2,000 feet below the surface of Crater Lake, God has walked. But out in the vast universe, beyond human sight, He has walked in deeper places than that. He has seen the tops of things and the bottom of things.

God is deeper than every problem we've ever wrestled with, deeper than any trouble in which we find ourselves. Before she died, Corrie ten Boom's sister Betsy told her, "There is no pit so deep that He is not deeper still." We can bring *any* situation to God and know that He daily deals with dilemmas far beyond the ones causing us grief or confusion. And the depth of His love makes Crater Lake seem like a shallow puddle on the sidewalk.

Lord, I'm in awe of You. My mind can't begin to grasp Your greatness. But thank You for the reminder that Your wisdom and love are far, far deeper than my problems.

★ ★ ★

GOD WANTS ME TO PLACE EVERY DETAIL OF EVERY
SITUATION I FACE INTO HIS HANDS—TRUSTING HIM
TO WORK IT OUT IN HIS WAY AND IN HIS TIME.

If you have enjoyed this book
or it has touched your life in some way,
we would love to hear from you.

Please send your comments to:
Hallmark Book Feedback
P.O. Box 419034
Mail Drop 100
Kansas City, MO 64141

Or e-mail us at:
booknotes@hallmark.com